Gaspard de la Nuit

Fantasies
in the manner of
Rembrandt and Callot

Gaspard de la Nuit

Fantasies
in the manner of
Rembrandt and Callot

by
Louis Bertrand

translated from the French
by
Gian Lombardo

Quale Press

Acknowledgement is made to the following magazines where some of the translations included here have previously appeared: lift, *The Prose Poem: An International Journal* and *Talisman*. "Haarlem" and "Moonlight" appeared in the anthology *Beginnings of the Prose Poem — All Over the Place*, edited by Mary Ann Caws and Michel Delville (Black Widow Press, 2021). "Mason," "Viol da Gamba," "My Great-Grandfather" and "Ondine" appeared in *Aloysius Bertrand's* Gaspard de la Nuit: *Beyond the Prose Poem,* by Valentina Gosetti (Legenda, 2016). Thanks are given to the editors of these publications. Versions of translations of Books I, II and III appeared as *Flemish School, Old Paris, & Night & Its Spells*, by Aloysius Bertrand (Quale Press *edition key satch(el)* Vol. 1, No. 1, 2000). Many thanks to Michel Delville and Christine Pagnoulle who helped answer some difficult questions on the original text.

Translation copyright © 2022 by Gian Lombardo

Drawings by Louis Bertrand courtesy of the Municipal Library of Angers (Angers, Bib. Mun. Rés. BL 1443 bis / © Ville d'Angers)

Collages by Bob Heman courtesy of the artist © 2022 by Bob Heman

Cover: *The Triumph of Time,* engraving by Philips Galle (1574), after Pieter Bruegel the Elder, courtesy of the Metropolitan Museum of Art

ISBN: 978-1-935835-29-5 trade paperback
       978-1-935835-30-1 hardcover

LCCN: 2022945767

Quale Press

www.quale.com

CONTENTS

GASPARD DE LA NUIT	XI
PREFACE	XXVII
TO M. VICTOR HUGO	XXXI

BOOK I. FLEMISH SCHOOL

I.	Haarlem	5
II.	Mason	9
III.	Captain Lazare	13
IV.	Pointed Beard	17
V.	Tulip Peddler	21
VI.	Five Fingers of the Hand	25
VII.	Viol da Gamba	29
VIII.	Alchemist	33
IX.	Setting Out for the Sabbath	37

Book II. Old Paris

I. Two Jews — 45
II. Night Tramps — 49
III. Lantern — 53
IV. Nesle Tower — 57
V. A Refined Person — 61
VI. Evening Prayers — 65
VII. Serenade — 69
VIII. Sir John — 73
IX. Midnight Mass — 77
X. Bibliophile — 81

Book III. Night and Its Spells

I. Gothic Chamber — 89
II. Scarbo — 93
III. Madman — 97
IV. Dwarf — 101
V. Moonlight — 105
VI. Patrol Beneath the Bell — 109
VII. Dream — 113
VIII. My Great-Grandfather — 117
IX. Ondine — 121
X. Salamander — 125
XI. Sabbath Hour — 129

BOOK IV. CHRONICLES
I.	Master Ogier	137
II.	Louvre Private Entrance	141
III.	The Flemish	145
IV.	The Hunt	149
V.	Black Riders	153
VI.	Illustrious Detachments	157
VII.	Lepers	165
VIII.	To a Bibliophile	169

BOOK V. SPAIN AND ITALY
I.	The Cell	177
II.	Mule Drivers	181
III.	Marquis D'Aroca	185
IV.	Henriquez	189
V.	The Alarm	193
VI.	Padre Pugnaccio	197
VII.	Masked Canto	201

BOOK VI. SYLPHS
I.	My Thatched Cottage	209
II.	River John	213
III.	October	217
IV.	On the Crags of Chèvremorte	221
V.	Another Spring	225
VI.	Second Man	229

To M. Charles Nodier	235
Notes	239
Translator's Afterword *by Gian Lombardo*	241
List of Illustrations	245

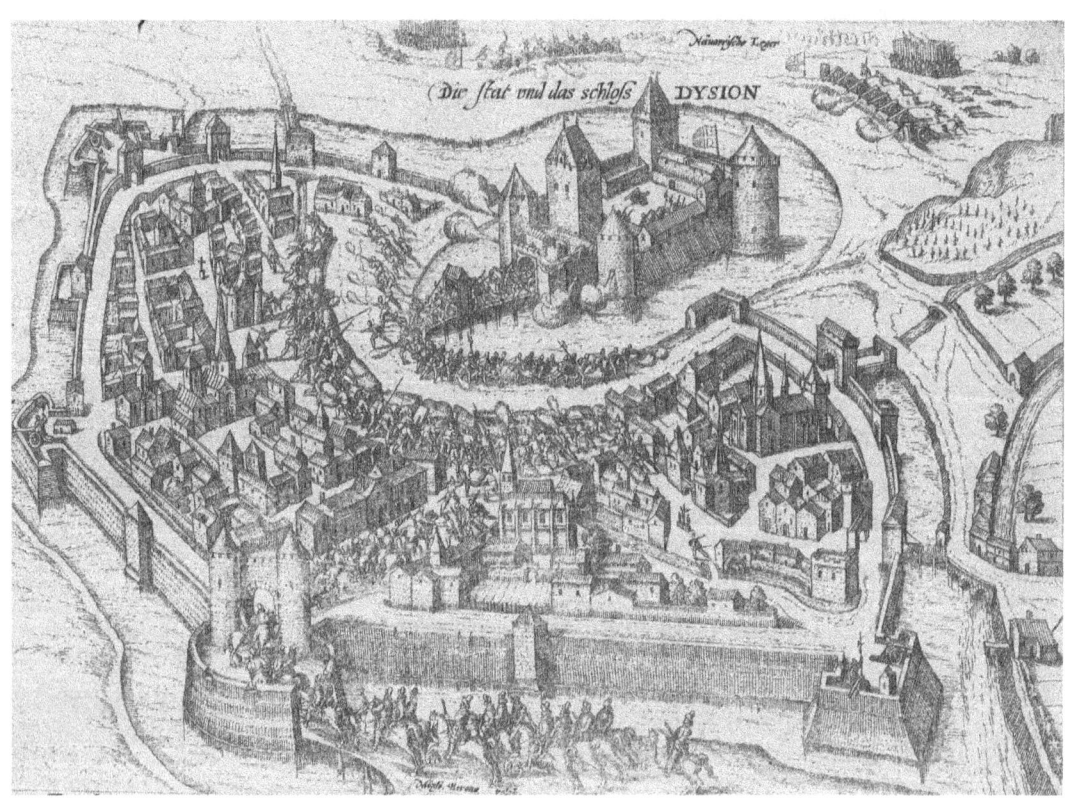

> Friend, do you remember while heading to Cologne,
> One Sunday, in Dijon, in the heart of Burgundy,
> We went about admiring steeples, gates and towers,
> And old houses hiding courtyards?
> SAINTE-BEUVE. *The Consolations.*

GASPARD DE LA NUIT

Gothic donjon
And Gothic spire*
From the sky's vantage,
Over there, it's Dijon.
Its cheery arbors,
Have no peer
Long ago its steeples
Were counted by tens.
There, more than one archway
Is scuplted or painted;
There, more than one gate
Opens like a fan.
Dijon, *Most tardy!***
And my pug-nosed lute
Sings of your mustard
and your Jacquemart!

I love Dijon like a child loves the nurse from whom he suckles milk, like the love a poet ignites in a maiden's heart. — Childhood and poetry! One's fleeting and the other's deceiving! Childhood's a butterfly in a hurry to burn her white wings on the flames of youth. And poetry's like the almond tree: its blossoms fragrant and fruit bitter.

*The keep of the palace of the dukes, and the spire of the cathedral, which travelers can make out several leagues distant in the plain.

**Moult me tarde! Old motto of the municipality of Dijon.

One day I was sitting by myself in the Garden of the Arquebus — a place named after the weapon where everyone knows the popinjay's men so often skillfully wielded them. Sitting quite still on a bench, you might be inclined to compare me to the statue of the Bastion Bazire. This masterpiece of the artisan Sevallée and painter Guillot depicted a priest sitting and reading. Nothing was out of place with his appearance. From a distance, he could be mistaken for a real person; closer up, you could see he's just plaster.

A passerby's cough dispelled my host of reveries. It was some poor devil whose outward demeanor proclaimed only misery and suffering. While in that garden, I had previously noticed his threadbare coat that was buttoned up to his chin, his shapeless felt cap no brush had ever groomed, his long willowy hair as tangled as undergrowth, his bony hands resembling something from an ossuary, his sneering visage, insidious and sickly, that tapered into a Nazarene's beard. And my fancies had charitably placed him among those small-time grifters, itinerant musicians and caricaturists whose insatiable hunger and unquenchable thirst condemn them to roam the world tracing the path of the Wandering Jew.

Now we're both on the same bench. My neighbor leafed through a book from whose pages a dried flower escaped without his knowing. I retrieved it for him. The stranger acknowledged me by bringing it to his withered lips and then replaced it in his mysterious book.

"This flower," I dared to say to him, "it's no doubt the token of some sweet, long-lost love? Alas! We've all endured a day that estranges us from the future!"

"You're a poet!" he replied, smiling.

The thread of our conversation had been set. Now what would commence emptying the spool?

"Poet, if being a poet means seeking art!"

"You sought art! And have you found it?"

"Hope to God that art were not a dream!"

"A dream! . . . And I too have sought it!" he cried with the vehemence of genius, and the pridefulness of triumph.

I begged him to show me by what eyepiece it might be discovered, art having been for me a needle in a haystack.

"I had resolved," he said, "to search for art in the same way medieval Rosicrucians sought the philosopher's stone — art, the nineteenth-century philosopher's stone!

"At first the question made me apply doctrines I had been schooled in. I wondered: What is art? — Art is the poet's science. — Definition as clear as a diamond in purest water.

"But what are the elements of art? — Second question I procrastinated for several months to tackle. — One evening as the lamp burned, as I dug through a bookseller's dusty coffers I unearthed a small book in a bizarre and unintelligible language whose title was embellished with a serpent uncoiling on a banner emblazoned with these two words: *Gott. Liebe.* A pittance was paid for this treasure. I ascended to my garret, and there, as I curiously thumbed through this puzzling book in front of my window bathed in moonlight, suddenly it seemed to me as if God's finger lightly grazed the keyboard of a universal organ, much like buzzing geometer moths emerging from amid the hearts of flowers swooning with delight from night's kisses on their lips. I stepped over to the window and looked down. Surprise! Was I dreaming? From a terrace that I had not noticed before wafted the exquisite emanations of orange trees. A young girl sat there, dressed in white, playing a harp, and an old man, dressed in black, knelt in prayer! — The book fell from my hand.

"I clambered down to greet the denizens of that terrace. The old man was a minister in the Reformed Church who had exchanged the cold of his Thuringian homeland for the exile of our warm Burgundy. The musician was his only child, a blond and frail beauty of seventeen who was being ravished by a slow-moving disease. And my book, which I had retrieved, was a German prayer book used in the Lutheran rite churches, and by the armies of the Prince of the House of Anhalt-Cöthen.

"'Ah! sir, do not stir still burning embers! Elizabeth is but a Beatrice in an azure dress. She's dead, sir, dead! And here's the prayer-book from which she set free her timorous prayer, the rose into which she exhaled her innocent soul. — She, another dried flower! — Closed book, like her destiny's book! — Blessed relics she cannot misapprehend for eternity, soaked in tears, when the trumpet of the archangel shatters my tombstone, I will hurtle through every realm until at last seated beside my beloved virgin under God's gaze!'"

"And art?" I asked him.

"What in art is *sentiment* comprised my unbearable grail. I loved, I prayed. *Gott. Liebe.* God and Love! — But what in art is *thought* still piqued my curiosity. I believed I'd find art's complement in nature; therefore, I contemplated nature.

"I left home in the morning and I did not return until evening. — Sometimes, leaning against the parapet of a fortress in ruins, I loved, for long stretches, to breathe the scent of wild and ubiquitous gillyflowers that dotted its golden bouquets among the coat of ivy along the walls of Louis XI's feudal and crumbling citadel;* to see a gust of wind, a sunbeam or a rainshower disturb the tranquil scene, the ortolan bunting and it chicks in the hedges play in the interchanging shadow and light of the garden, thrushes flock

---

*This castle, imposed on Dijon by Louis XI's tyrannical mistrust, when after the death of Charles the Bold he seized the duchy to the detriment of the legitimate heiress Marie of Burgundy, has more than once fired upon the city, which, it is true, did graciously return fire. Today, its ancient towers serve as barracks for a company of gendarmes.

from the mountain to harvest the vineyard tall and dense enough to hide the fabled stag, crows swoop down from every part of the sky in weary packs onto the carcass of a horse abandoned by the *skinner** in a verdant ditch; to listen to the tongue-wagging washerwomen who were sounding their happy *pounding* of clothes on the banks of the Suzon** and to a child sing a mournful tune while spinning the ropemaker's wheel at the foot of the city's great wall. — Sometimes in my daydreams I blazed a mossy and dew-laden path, silent and peaceful, far from the city. How often have I filched from distaffs of red and tart fruit in mostly forgotten thickets bordering the spring of youth and the hermitage of Notre-Dame-d'Etang,*** the fountain of spirits and fairies, the hermitage of the Devil! How many times have I picked up a petrified whelk and fossilized coral on the stony hills of St. Joseph gullied by storms! How many times have I caught crayfish in the rushing fords of the Tilles,† among the watercress where the cold-blooded salamander lives, and among the water lilies, those yawning lazy flowers! How many times have I spied on a grass snake mired in muck in Saulons, hearing only the coot's plaintive cry, and the grebe's funereal moan! How many times have I starred with a candle the underground caves in Asnières where stalactites distill slowly drop by drop the eternal hourglass of the centuries! How many times have

---

*Pialey, a flayer of dead horses.

**Torrent that once ran through Dijon out in the open. Nowadays, its waters flow into vaulted canals at the foot of the city ramparts. — *Val-de-Suzon* trout are famous in Burgundy.

***The now closed chapel of Notre-Dame-d'Étang was inhabited in 1630 by a chaplain and a hermit. Since the latter murdered his colleague, a ruling by the parliament of Dijon condemned him to be beaten alive in Place Morimont.

†Generic name of several small rivers that provide water for the country of the plain, between Dijon and the Saône.

I blasted a horn atop the sheer face of Chèvremorte, the stagecoach struggling up the path to three hundred feet below my misty throne! And even those nights, those summer nights, balmy and hazy, how many times have I jigged like a lycanthrope around a fire that lights up the grassy and untenanted valley until the first blows of the woodcutter's axe sets oaks shaking! — Ah! sir, how solitude has charms for the poet! I would have been happy to live in the forest, and not make more noise than a bird drinking at a spring, than a bee nibbling at hawthorn and whose proboscis once inserted into a blossom bursts it!"

"And art?" I asked him.
"Patience! — Art was still in limbo. I studied the spectacle of nature. I studied next the monuments of men.
"Dijon has not always blessed its leisure time with concerts by its philharmonic progeny. She has shouldered the hauberk — donned the morion helmet — brandished the pike — unsheathed the sword — loaded the arquebus — aimed the cannon on its ramparts — charged across fields with drums beating and banners unravelled — and, like the gray-bearded minstrel who before strumming his rebec leads off with a trumpet blast, she would have some wonderful war stories to tell; or rather — her crumbling bastions that encase webs of horse chestnut roots in earth mixed with shards — and her decrepit castle whose drawbridge trembles under the weary step of the constable's mare returning to the barracks — all testify to two Dijons — a Dijon of today, a Dijon of old.
"I had quickly dispensed with the Dijon of the fourteenth and fifteenth centuries, around which ran an arc of eighteen towers and eight gates and four auxiliary gates, or posterns — the Dijon of Philippe the Bold, Jean the Fearless, Philippe the Good, Charles the Rash — with its cob houses, with pointed gables like fool's caps, with façades criss-crossed with St. Andrew's

crosses, with fortified mansions, narrow gates, double wickets, and courtyards lined with halberds — with her churches, her most holy chapel, abbeys, monasteries, that formed cavalcades of belfries, spires, steeples, unfurling like banners their gold and azure windows, arraying their miraculous relics, kneeling at the dark crypts of their martyrs, or within flowered nooks in their gardens — with her torrent the Suzon whose course, laden with wooden bridges and flour mills, separated the territory of the abbot of St. Bénigne from the territory of the abbot of St. Étienne, in the same way a sargeant-at-arms in parliament throws his staff and his foot down between two litigants swollen with anger.* — And finally, with its populous suburbs, of which one, that of St. Nicolas, showed its dozen streets in the sun, no more or less than like a fat sow showing her twelve teats. — I had galvanized a corpse and the corpse had risen.

"Dijon wakes; rises, walks, runs! — Thirty little bell towers ring in an ultramarine blue sky, just as old Albert Dürer painted. The crowd throngs at inns on rue Bouchepot, at the Porte aux Chanoines public baths, at the stalls on rue St. Guillaume, at the exchange on rue Notre-Dame, at the arms factories on rue des Forges, at the fountain at Place des Cordeliers, at the community oven on rue de Bèze, at the covered market at Place Champeaux, at the gallows on Place Morimont. — The upper crust, nobles, villains, hired gangsters, priests, monks, clerics, merchants, varlets, Jews, Lombards, pilgrims, minstrels, officers of parliament and the budget

---

*The two abbeys of St. Étienne and St. Bénigne, whose disputes so often tried the patience of parliament, were so ancient, so powerful, and enjoyed so many privileges granted by dukes and popes, that there was no religious establishment that did not fall under one or the other. The seven churches in the city were their daughters, and each of the two abbeys also had its own particular church. — The Abbey of St. Étienne even minted its own money.

office, tax collectors, officers of the duke's household: who cry out, who whistle, who sing, who complain, who pray, who curse — in ox carts, in litters, on horseback, on mules, on St. François's hackneys. — And how can we doubt this resurrection? See how the silk standard flutters in the wind, half green, half yellow, embroidered with the city's coat of arms, which are heraldic red with a vine of gold leafed with green.*

"But what's this cavalcade? It's the Duke who's going to have a delightful time hunting. The Duchess has already preceded him to his castle at Rouvres. — A magnificent showing and a never-ending procession! — His Lordship the Duke spurs his dapple gray mare that shivers in the crisp, sharp morning air. Behind him prance and strut the *Wealthy* of Châlons, the *Fine Blood* of Vienne, the *Dashing* from Vergy, Neuchâtel's *Pride*, the *Good Barons* of Beaufremont. — And those two characters straggling at the tail end of the queue? The youngest, as distinguished by his lovely ox-blood velvet riding jacket and his jangling sceptre, roars with laughter; the older, dressed in a black cloth cloak from under which he withdraws a voluminous psalter, bows his head diffidently: one is King of Ribalds, the other the Duke's chaplain.** The fool badgers the wise man with questions that the latter cannot answer; and meanwhile the populace shouts: "Blessings!" — May the palfreys neigh, may the bloodhounds bay, may the horns blare; they, with the reins on the necks of their ambling

---

*Such would have been, according to Pierre Paillot, the old coat of arms of the municipality of Dijon, but Abbé Boulemier (*Memoir of the Academy of Dijon*, 1771) claimed that they were only *just red*. Are these two scholars confused about dates? The coat of arms of Dijon would not have been solely red before bearing the gold vine leafed with green. But I don't have time to fully delve into that issue here.

**Philippe the Bold had his *King of Ribalds*. He gave him 200 livres in 1396 (*Courtépée*).

horses, chat familiarly about the politic lady Judith and the gallant Maccabaeus.

"Meantime, a herald blows on a conch shell from the tower of the duke's castle. He lets the hunters out in the country know that they can let loose their falcons. — The weather turns rainy; in the distance a grayish mist hides from him the Abbey of Citeaux, with its woods dappled with marshes. However, a ray of sunlight unveils to him — closer and more distinctly — the Castle of Talant, whose terraces and platforms crenellated the tableau — the manors of the lords of Ventoux and Fontaine, whose weathervanes punctuate massive swathes of greenery — the monastery of St. Maur whose dovecotes become fully outlined against a flock of pigeons — the leper colony of St. Apollinaire that has only one door and no windows — the chapel of St. Jacques of Trimolois, which resembles a pilgrim bedecked with shells — and below the walls of Dijon, beyond the Abbey of St. Bénigne's farm, the cloister of the Charterhouse, white as the frock of disciples of St. Bruno.

"The Charterhouse of Dijon! The St. Denis of the Dukes of Burgundy!* — Ah! why should children be jealous of the masterworks of their fathers! — Now go to where the Charterhouse use to lie, your footsteps will strike there beneath the grass slabs that used to be keystones, altar tabernacles, tombstones, oratory flagstones — stones that had been immersed in the smoke of incense, where wax has

---

*I only compare the Charterhouse of Dijon to the Abbey of St. Denis in relation to the magnificence and the richness of its sepulchers. Only three dukes were buried at the Charterhouse: Philippe the Bold, Jean the Fearless, and Philippe the Good, and I am not unaware that the Church of Citeaux had commonly received, since Eudes the First, the spoils of the dukes from the first and second royal houses. — It is Philippe the Bold who founded the Charterhouse in 1383. Everything throughout was made of expensive imported oak panelling, with chasubles and carpets woven from golden cloth, curtains from fabrics from Cyprus and Damascus,

been burned, where the organ has sounded, where living dukes have knelt, where dead dukes have lain their heads. — O unto nothingness have become greatness and glory! Gourds are planted in the ashes of Philippe the Bold! — No more Charterhouse! — But I'm wrong — the great door of the church and its bell tower still stand; the slender and delicate turret, like a small bouquet of gillyflowers on an ear, looks like a young man leading a greyhound on a leash; the hammered door would be another jewel to hang around the neck of a cathedral. Besides that there's — in the courtyard of the cloister — a huge pedestal missing its cross and around which are nestled six statues of prophets — impressive even in their desolation. And why do they cry? They mourn the cross the angels carried back to heaven.

"The fate of the Charterhouse was the same as most of the monuments that adorned Dijon at the time when the duchy was reincorporated into the royal domain. This city is only a shadow of herself. Louis XI stripped her of her power; the Revolution beheaded her steeples. She only has three of seven churches remaining, with one holy chapel,* two abbeys and a dozen monasteries. Three of her gates are useless, her smaller gates have been razed, her outlying districts leveled, her torrent — the Suzon — channeled into sewers, her people terrorized to

---

with silver holy water fonts and candlesticks, vermeil lamps, portable altars with ivory figurines, with paintings and sculptures executed by the foremost artists of the time. The platters for the altar service weighed 55 marks. — The hammer of the Revolution destroyed the Charterhouse, flinging into the hands of a few collectors shards from the tombs of Philippe the Bold, Jean the Fearless and his last wife Marguerite of Bavaria. (Charles the Rash did not erect any sort of monument to his father Philippe the Good.) These masterpieces of the art of fifteenth century have been restored and placed in one of the rooms of the Dijon museum.

*It has not escaped any better from the fury of people and time than the Charterhouse and so many other fine edifaces. No stone left upon another. This holy chapel, built by Duke Hugues III on his return from

the core, and her nobility fallen to the distaff. — Alas! we can see that Duke Charles and his legions of cavalry that departed — already four centuries ago* — for battle, still not have not returned.

"And me? I wandered among these ruins like an antique hunter scrounging for Roman medals in the furrows of a *castrum* after a wild thunderstorm. Dear-departed Dijon still retains something of her former self, like those rich Gauls who were buried with a piece of gold in their mouths and another clutched in their right hands."

"And art?" I asked him.

"I was busy one day, in front of our Notre-Dame, contemplating Jacquemart, his wife and child, slamming the noon hour. — Jacquemart's punctuality, his earnestness, his stolidness would testify to his Flemish origin, even if we did not know that he rang out the hours to the good folk of Kortrijk during the sack of that city in 1383. Gargantua swiped the bells of Paris, Philippe the Bold the clock of Kortrijk; each prince according to his stature. — A flurry of laughter was heard from up there and I saw, in one corner of the Gothic building, one of those monstrous figures that medieval sculptors attached by the shoulders to the eaves of the cathedrals; an atrocious figure of the damned who, in the midst of suffering, stuck out his tongue, gnashed his teeth and wrung his hands. — It was he who had laughed."

---

a crusade, around 1171, was rich with a thousand works of art and faith. What has become of, for example, its stained-glass windows and its historical statues; the choir paneling where hung the coat of arms of the thirty-one foremost Knights of the Golden Fleece founded by Philippe the Good; the beautiful chalice where was kept the miraculous host and on which shone, on feast days, the golden crown that King Louis XII, recovering from a dangerous illness in 1505, had sent to the order by two heralds? — Time takes a step forward and the earth is renewed, says M. de Chateaubriand somewhere.

*Charles the Rash, last Duke of Burgundy, was killed at the Battle of Nancy, Sunday, January 5, 1476.

"You had something in your eye!" I cried.

"Nothing in my eye, nor cotton in my ear. — The stone figure laughed — laughed with a maniacal, frightful, infernal laugh — sarcastic, cutting, blood curdling."

I felt ashamed with myself for spending so much time conversing with a monomaniac. However, with a smile I encouraged this Rosicrucian in art to continue his entertaining story.

"This adventure," he went on, "made me reflect. — I reflected that since God and love were the founding conditions for art, what in art comprises *feeling*. — Satan could well be the second of these conditions, what in art is *thought*. — Didn't the Devil build Cologne Cathedral?

"Here I am in search of the Devil. My face drained of color as I perused the magic books of Cornelius Agrippa and I slit the throat of my schoolmaster neighbour's black hen. — No more the Devil than the final bead of a devotee's rosary! Yet he exists. — St. Augustine has, with his pen, validated this description: *Daemones sunt genere animalia, ingenio rationabilia, animo passiva, corpore aerea, tempore aeterna*. That's certain. The Devil exists. He takes the floor in the Chamber of Deputies, he pleads in the Palace of Justice, he hollers at the Stock Exchange. We sketch him in drawings, we bind him into novels, we dress him in dramas. We see him everywhere, just as I see you here, right now. Pocket mirrors were invented so that he'd have an easier time trimming his beard. Punchinello missed his enemy and ours. Oh! why didn't he knock him out with a smack to the back of his neck!

"I drank Paracelsus's potion in the evening before going to bed. I had the colic. Nowhere does the Devil with horns and tail appear.

"Another disappointment: — the storm that night wet the old city to her bones as she curled up sleeping. Yet I crept about, gropingly, not minding the drops, in the nooks and crannies of Notre-Dame. One might call it sacrilege.

There's no lock to which crime does not have the key. —
Have mercy on me! I had need of a host and a relic. — A
light pierced the darkness. Many others appeared in succession, so that I soon distinguished someone whose bony hand with a long taper was distributing the flame to the candles atop the altar. It was Jacquemart who, no less imperturbable as usual under his patched iron *hood*, finished his task without seeming to be bothered or even noticing the presence of a lay witness. Jacqueline, kneeling on the steps, maintained a perfect stillness, the rain flowing from her Brabant-fashion lead skirt, with her wimple made of tin tipped like Bruges lace, her face of varnished wood like the cheeks of a Nuremberg doll. I stuttered a humble question about the Devil and art to her when the Maritorne's arms sprung wide open from the sudden and brutal release of a coiled spring, and, from the noise a hundred times echoed from the heavy hammer that she clenched with her fist, a crowd of abbots, knights, patrons who populate with their Gothic mummies the Gothic sepulchers of the church flowed processionally around the dazzling altar with its life-like and angelic display of a Christmas pageant's manger. The black virgin,* the virgin from barbarian times, a yard tall, with the glistening crown of gold latticework, with her dress stiff from starch and pearls, the miraculous virgin before whom hisses a silver lamp, leapt from her throne and ran across the flagstones with speed of a flying top. She proceeded from the remotest naves, with graceful and uneven leaps, accompanied by a tiny St. Jean of wax and wool set afire by a spark and melted blue and red. Jacqueline had armed herself with scissors to trim the back of her swaddled child's head; a candle lit up the baptistery chapel in the distance, and then. . ."

---

*This icon was already in great veneration in the XIIth century. It was shaped from a dark wood, hard and heavy, that is believed to be chestnut.

"Then what?"

"And then the sun that shone through a narrow opening, the sparrows that pecked at my windowpanes, and the bells that murmured a verse from the clouds woke me. I had had a dream."

"And the Devil?"

"He doesn't exist."

"And art?"

"Exists."

"But where?"

"In God's heart!" — And his eye, where a tear had sprung, plumbed the heavens. — "We are, ourselves, sir, only the Creator's copyists. The most magnificent, most triumphant, most glorious of our ephemeral works is never more than an unworthy counterfeit, nothing more than the muddied radiance from the least of His immortal creations. Any originality is but an eaglet that breaks the shell of its egg in the sublime and sunlit eyries of the Sinai. — Yes, sir, I have long sought pure art! O delirium! O madness! Look at this forehead wrinkled by the iron crown of woe! Thirty years! And the mystery that I pleaded for during so many unrelenting vigils, to whom I've sacrificed youth, love, pleasure, fortune, the mystery lies, inert and lifeless, like some revolting dropping, in the ashes of my illusions! Nothingness does not but give life to nothingness."

He started to get up. I conveyed my sympathy to him with a hypocritical and banal sigh.

"This manuscript," he added, "will tell you how many instruments my lips have tested before I happened on the one that makes a pure and expressive note, how many brushes I used on the canvas before seeing the dawn of chiaroscuro born there. There are recorded various theories, perhaps novel ones, of harmony and color, from which my rantings would have obtained the only result and the only reward. Read it; return it to me tomorrow. The cathedral bell tolls six o'clock; these hours chase the sunlight that creeps along these lilacs. I'm going to shut myself up to write my will. Good evening."

"Sir!"

Damn! He had gotten too far away. I remained as still and embarrassed as a manager whose clerk had pointed out a flea riding on his managerial nose. The manuscript was entitled: GASPARD DE LA NUIT. *Fantasies in the manner of Rembrandt and Callot.*

The next day was a Saturday. No one at the *Arquebuse*; a few Jews were observing their Sabbath. I ran about the city asking each passerby about M. Gaspard de la Nuit, our Mr. Night's Guardian, our Mr. Keeper of the Night, our Night's Treasurer, our dear, scurrying rat. Some answered me: — "Oh! you're joking!" — Others: "Well, I hope he wrings your neck!" — And all quickly scattered from me. I approached a vintner from *rue St. Felebar*, a hunchback dwarf, who sat on his stoop laughing at my predicament.

"Do you know M. Gaspard de la Nuit?"

"What do you want with that guy?"

"I want to give him back a book he lent me."

"A book of black magic!"

"What? Black magic? . . . I beg you show me where he lives."

"Over there, where that claw-head knocker hangs."

"But that house. . . You're directing me to the parish priest."

"It's because I just saw a tall brunette go into his house who washes his albs and his rabats."

"What do you mean?"

"I mean that M. Gaspard de la Nuit sometimes decks himself out as a young and pretty girl to tempt devout folk — note his business with St. Antoine, my patron saint."

"Spare me your impertinence and tell me where's M. Gaspard de la Nuit."

"He's in hell, assuming he's nowhere else."

"Ah! I'm finally getting it! What? Gaspard de la Nuit then would be . . . ?"

"Him? Yes. . . The Devil!"

"Thank you, my good fellow! . . . If Gaspard de la Nuit is in hell, let him roast there! I'm publishing his book."

LOUIS BERTRAND.

PREFACE.

« XXVII »

PREFACE

Art's a coin with two antithetic faces. For example, one side reveals a face resembling Paul Rembrandt and the reverse that of Jacques Callot. — Rembrandt is a philosopher with a white beard who's like a snail winding into its shell, whose thought emerges from meditation and prayer, who closes his eyes in order to commune with himself, who is sustained by the spirits of beauty, science, wisdom and love, and who consumes himself in penetrating nature's mysterious manifestations. — Callot, on the other hand, is a blustering and obscene infantryman who struts about town, who kicks up a stir in the tavern, who fondles loose women, who swears only by his rapier and his blunderbuss, and whose only vexation is having to wax his moustache. — While the author of this book has viewed art under this double personification he does not want to be too exclusive. Therefore, here are, besides fantasies in the manner of Rembrandt and Callot, some studies of Van Eyck, Lucas de Leyde, Albert Dürer, Peeter Neef, Breughel de Velours, Breughel d'Enfer, Van Ostade, Gérard Dow, Salvator-Rosa, Murillo, Fusely, as well as some other masters from different schools.

Also, if the author is asked why he hasn't gotten it into his head to model this book on some noble literary theory, he will be forced to reply that M. Séraphin does not explain the mechanism of his shadow puppets, and that Punchinello hides from the curious crowd the guide wires strung to his arms. — And so he is content to sign his work

GASPARD DE LA NUIT.

TO M. VICTOR HUGO.

« XXXI »

Glory does not know my secret abode,
And I sing my sorrowful song all alone,
Which has charm only for me.
  Ch. Brugnot. *Ode.*

"Who cares about your wandering spirits," said Adam, "I worry about them no more than an eagle worries about a flock of wild geese. All those beings have fled since the pulpits have been seized by brave ministers, and the people's ears filled with holy doctrines."
  Walter Scott. *The Abbot*, chap. XVI.

TO M. VICTOR HUGO

That charming book of your verses, in a hundred years as well as today, will be very much esteemed by lords, damsels and minstrels — an anthology of chivalry, a decameron of love that will charm those nobles in their fine castles.

But this little book that I dedicate to you will have suffered the fate of everything that dies, after having, one morning perhaps, amused the court and the city who are amused by piddling trifles.

Anyhow, if a bibliophile dares to exhume this moldy and worm-eaten work, he will read on the first page your illustrious name which won't save mine from oblivion.

His curiosity will liberate the pathetic miasma of my thoughts that will have been imprisoned for so long in the vermeil coverings of a parchment prison.

And this discovery will be no less precious for him than for us, happening upon some inscription in Gothic letters, adorned with a unicorn or a couple storks.

Paris, 20 September 1836.

The Fantasies Of Gaspard de la Nuit

HERE BEGINS THE FIRST
BOOK OF THE FANTASIES
OF GASPARD
DE LA
NUIT.

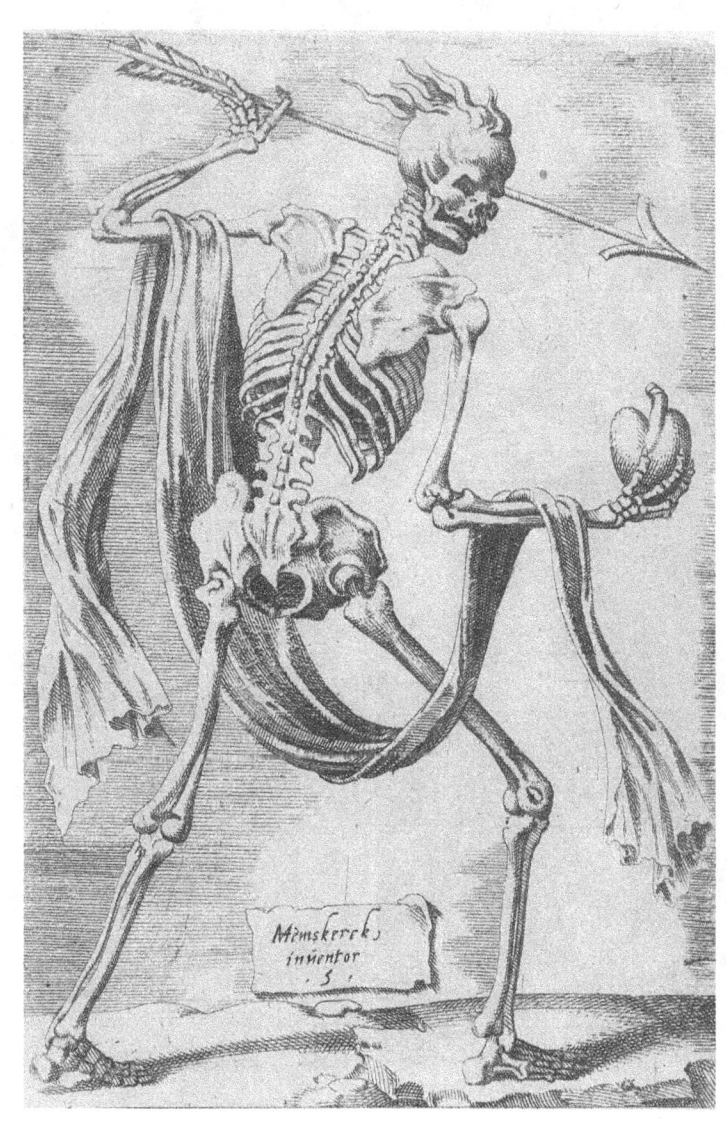

FLEMISH SCHOOL

HAARLEM

I.

When Amsterdam's golden cock sings, Haarlem's golden hen lays an egg.
The Centuries by NOSTRADAMUS.

HAARLEM

Haarlem, that marvellous grotesquerie epitomizing the Flemish school. Haarlem as painted by Jan Breughel, Peeter Neef, David Téniers and Paul Rembrandt.

Where blue water ripples in its canals, and where church windows glaze almost golden. Where linen dangles from stoëls,* drying in the sun, and roofs everywhere green with straw.

And, flapping their wings, storks circle the town clock, stretch their necks straight into the wind and catch raindrops in their beaks.

And the burgomaster, who rarely gives anything much thought, rubs his double chin, and the lovelorn flower girl slowly wastes away, her gaze not wavering from one of her tulips.

And a minstrel swoons, buckling over her mandolin, and an old man plays a rommelpot,** and some kid inflates a bladder, eager to begin his game.

And drinkers smoke in a murky dive, and a maid hangs a dead pheasant in a tavern window.

* Stone balconies.
**A musical instrument.

MASON

II.

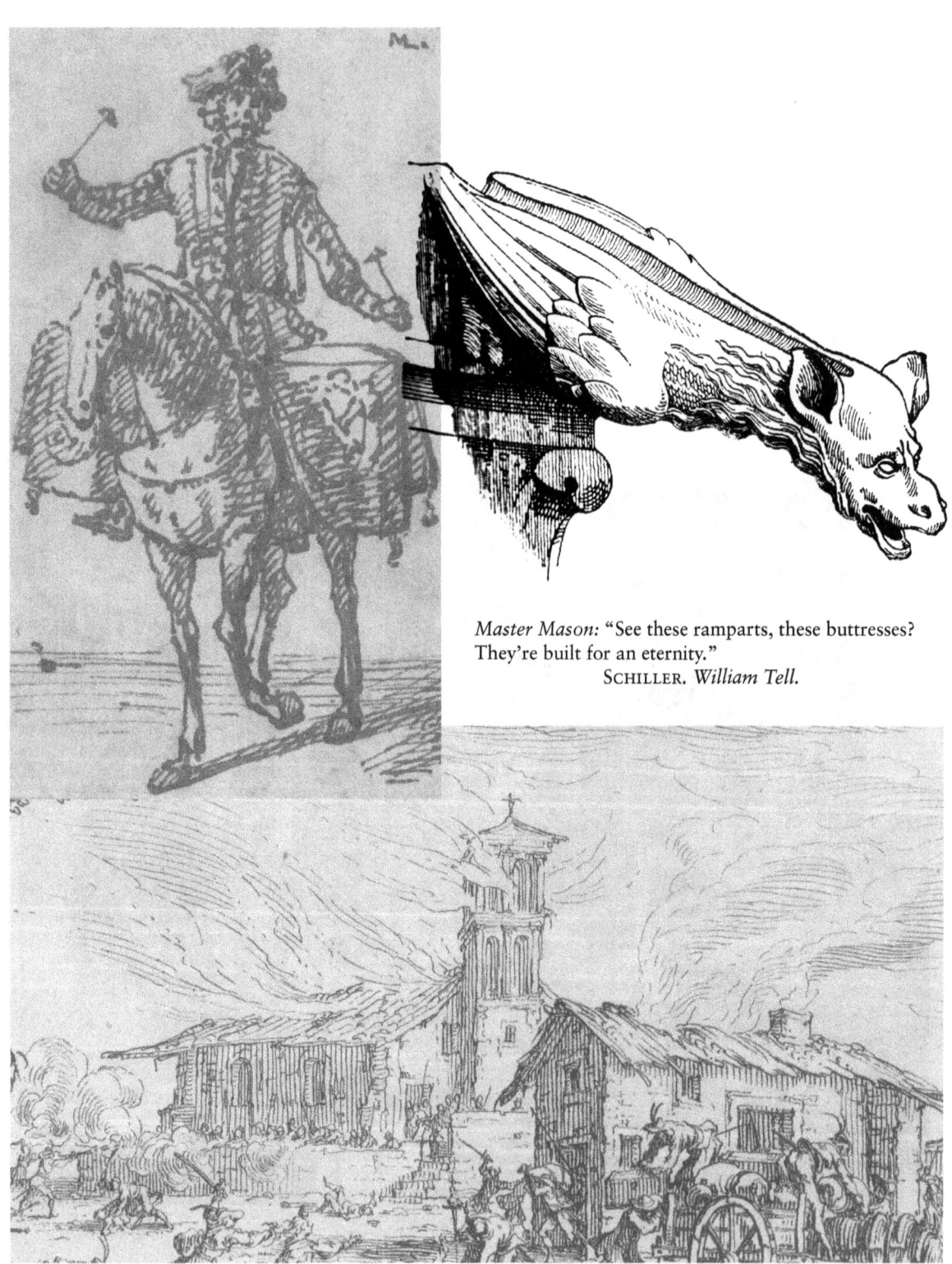

Master Mason: "See these ramparts, these buttresses? They're built for an eternity."
        SCHILLER. *William Tell.*

MASON

The mason Abraham Knupfer sings, trowel in hand, on top of his scaffold way up in the air — he's up so high that he can read the Gothic inscriptions on the great church bell — his feet leveling the thirty flying buttresses of the church, as well as the whole town with its thirty churches.

He sees gargoyles spew water from roof-slates into a jumbled chasm of balconies, windows, pendants, spires, towers, roofs and house frames, which the motionless and scalloped falcon's wing taints with a grey speck.

He sees fortifications arrayed like stars in the sky, the citadel sticking out like a hen's head poking from a pot pie, rows of palaces with fountains dried up by the sun, and cloisters where shadows swing round and round the pillars.

The king's guard has encamped in the outskirts of town. Look! A horseman's drumming there. Abraham Knupfer espies his tricorn hat, his red woolen aiguillettes, his cockade banded by braid, and his pigtail tied with a ribbon.

That's not all he sees, though. There's a bunch of soldiers in the park. Under its great, green boughs and on its broad, emerald lawns they riddle a wooden bird nailed atop a maypole with shots from their arquebuses.

And, come evening, while the nave slumbers in deep harmony, recumbent with arms crossed, from his ladder he catches sight of a village on the horizon set aflame by men at war, blazing like a comet in the azure.

CAPTAIN LAZARE

III.

"Too many precautions can't be taken these days, since, most importantly, counterfeiters have settled in our midst."
Seige of Berg-Op-Zoom.

CAPTAIN LAZARE

He sits in his Utrecht velour armchair, *the* Johan Blazius, while the clock of St. Paul's church chimes noon across the bug-infested, sooty roofs of the neighborhood.

He sits down at his counter of the finest imported oak, the gouty Lombard, to change this golden ducat that I pull from my puffy pants — one hot fart.

One of two thousand that a bloody ricochet of fortune and war cast from the purse of a Benedictine friar into the purse of a captain of the Lansquenet!

God help me! The dunce examines it through his magnifying glass and weighs it with his assay balance, as if my sword had minted counterfeit money on the monk's skull!

Now, let's get a move on, Mister Cuckold. I have neither the inclination nor the energy to chase away those johns over there to whom your wife has just thrown a bouquet through this casement.

And I need to down a few tankards — bored and downhearted, since the peace of Munster has imprisoned me in this castle like a rat in a trap.

POINTED BEARD

IV.

If one doesn't strut, chin held high,
Have one's beard curled,
And moustache brushed stiff,
One is mistaken for a woman.
　　　　Poetry of D'Assoucy.

POINTED BEARD

Solemn services were being held at the synagogue. Its somber interior was starred with the lights of silver lamps. The rabbis, in robes and pince-nezs, kissed their Talmuds, muttered, spat or blew their noses. Some were seated, others not.

And, there, all of a sudden, in the midst of so many rounded, oval and square curly beards that shed small, white flecks and powder, and exhaled amber and benjamin, a beard trimmed to a point was spotted.

An old, venerable scholar by the name of Elebotham, crowned with a flannel turban that glittered with small gems, stood up and cried: — "Blasphemy! Someone's got a pointed beard here!"

"A Lutheran beard!" — "A short cloak. Naked in the sight of the Lord!" — "Kill the Philistine!" — And the crowd stamped their feet angrily, raising a commotion in the pews as the officiating rabbi brayed: — "Samson, give me your jawbone of an ass!"

Melchior the knight unrolled a parchment authenticated with the state seal: — "This is a writ," he read, "to arrest the butcher Isaac van Heck so that the assassin can be hung between two Flemish swine."

The sound of heavy footsteps and the clinking of metal against metal came from the shadowed corridor. Thirty halberdiers crashed into the room. — "The Devil take your halberds!" — Isaac the butcher sneered. And, then, he jumped out a window into the Rhine.

TULIP PEDDLER

V.

Among flowers, the tulip is what the peacock is among birds. One is without fragrance, the other without voice. One is proud of its robe, the other of its tail.
The Garden of Rare and Curious Flowers.

TULIP PEDDLER

No sound, except for the rumpling of two vellum pages between the scholar Huylten's fingertips who only looked up from the pages of his Bible decorated with Gothic illuminations to admire the gold and purple of two fish held captive on the label of a druggist's bottle.

Knocking sounds rolled up from the door and a flower peddler, his arms laden with several pots of tulips, apologized for interrupting such a learned man's reading.

"Master," he said, "behold the treasure of treasures, the wonder of wonders! Why only one bulb such as this ever flowers each century in the Emperor of Constantinople's seraglio!"

"A tulip!" cried the irritated old man. "A tulip! Symbol of man's pride and lust which produced Luther's and Melanchthon's odious heresies in the unfortunate city of Wittenberg!"

Master Huylten fastened the clasp of his Bible, put his spectacles in their case, and drew open the drapes. The sunlight enabled him to view a passion flower with its crown of thorns, its sponge, its lash, its spikes and the five wounds of Our Lord.

The tulip peddler knelt reverently and silently, overcome by an inquisitorial stare from the Duke of Albe whose portrait — a Holbein masterpiece — had been hung on the wall.

FIVE FINGERS OF THE HAND

VI.

An honest family where there had never been a bankruptcy, where no one had ever been hanged.
The Family History of Jean de Nivelle.

FIVE FINGERS OF THE HAND

The thumb's this fat, Flemish barkeep, a lewd and sarcastic man who stands, smoking, in his doorway beneath a signboard depicting the trademark of doubly-potent bock beer.

The index finger's his wife, a shrew dry as salt cod who, from morning to night, thrashes the maid out of jealousy and caresses the bottle out of love.

The middle finger's their son, a rough, axe-hewn fellow who would have been a soldier if he didn't have to stand behind a bar, and who would have been a horse if he weren't already a man.

Their daughter's the ring finger, the lively and enticing Zerbine who sells lace to the ladies, but is loath to sell her smiles to the gentlemen.

And the pinkie's the family pet, a little, sniveling monkey who waddles around, forever clutching mama's dress, dangling from her waist — a baby impaled on an ogress' fangs.

The five fingers of this hand bruise the most delightful five-petaled gillyflower that ever embroidered the flower gardens of the noble city of Haarlem.

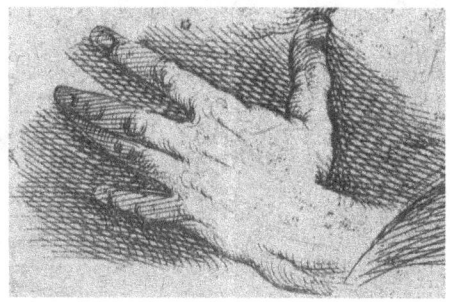

VIOL DA GAMBA

VII.

He recognized, without doubt, the pale visage of his dear friend Jean-Gaspard Debureau, the best clown in the Funambule Theater. As he stared at it, an expression of indescribable malice and amusement rose on his face.
    THEOPHILE GAUTIER. *Onuphrius.*

    My good friend Pierrot
    Lend me your quill
    So I can write a word or two
    Under the light of the moon.
    My candle's gone out.
    There's not a light in the house.
    For the love of God, Pierrot,
    Open your door.
      Popular Song.

VIOL DA GAMBA

The choirmaster had hardly begun interrogating a viola, drawing his bow across its humming body, when it answered him with the jeers and catcalls more often heard at a burlesque. It seemed that a particular indigestion from too much exposure to slapstick had lodged in its belly.

*

First, Barbara, the chaperone, bawled out that sap Pierrot, that klutz, for dropping the box containing M. Cassandre's wig, flinging powder all over the place.

And, with such a crushed look on his face, M. Cassandre picked up his wig, and Harlequin gave the blockhead a swift kick in the ass, and Colombine laughed so hard she had to wipe a tear from her eye, and Pierrot let loose a white painted clown's grin that stretched from ear to ear.

But, not long after this, beneath a full moon, Harlequin begged his friend Pierrot to unlock his door so he could give him something to light his candle. The old man stood there whining at the door even though the bastard had made off with his young lady, not to mention his money.

*

"The Devil take Job Hans, that good-for-nothing lute-maker, who sold me this bowstring!" the choirmaster exclaimed as he placed the dusty viola back in its dusty case. — The bowstring had busted.

ALCHEMIST

VIII.

    Our art is learned in two ways: First, through the teachings of a master, from mouth to mouth and not otherwise, or through divine revelation; and, second, through very obscure and muddled texts. In order to find truth and concordance in these texts one must be cunning, patient, studious and vigilant.
    The Key to the Secrets of Philosophy, by Pierre Vicot.

ALCHEMIST

Nothing yet! — And I've spent the last three days and nights under the dim light of this lamp, pouring over Lulle's most hermetic texts.

No, nothing, only jeers from the stove incessantly making a game of disturbing my thoughts — that and the hissing from the glittering retort.

Sometimes that furnace hurls a flaming dart from its trap that lands on my cloak, or, sometimes, it flings a spark onto a tuft of my beard.

Or else it fires up so hot its casings glow and ashes flurry over the pages of my formulary and the ink on my desk.

And the retort, glittering ever so much more, whistles the Devil's own tune whenever St. Eloy in his forge grabs its barrel nose with his pincers.

But nothing yet! — And I'll spend another three days and nights under the dim light of this lamp, pouring over Lulle's most hermetic texts.

SETTING OUT FOR THE SABBATH

IX.

When she rose, she brought night with her. And, lighting a candle, she grabbed a bottle and annointed herself. Then, after speaking a few words, she was transported to the witches' Sabbath.
     JEAN BODIN. *Demonomania of Sorcerers.*

SETTING OUT FOR THE SABBATH

A dozen of them ate beer soup from a coffin; every one of them using a dead man's forearm for a spoon.

The fireplace glowed red with embers. As candles burned they formed wax mushrooms in the smoke and crockery exuded a fragrance not unlike the smell of graves in springtime.

And, whenever Maribas laughed or cried, it was like hearing a bow scrape over the strings of a broken violin.

The old buzzard cackled as he brought out and placed on the table, beside a flickering candle, a book of spells upon which a scorched fly fell.

This fly was still buzzing when a spider, dragging its great, hairy belly, scaled the edges of the magic tome.

But the warlocks and witches had already fled up the chimney astride brooms and pokers and other fireplace utensils, and Maribas, certainly not the least among them, on the handle of a frying pan.

HERE ENDS THE FIRST
BOOK OF THE FANTASIES
OF GASPARD
DE LA
NUIT.

HERE BEGINS THE SECOND
BOOK OF THE FANTASIES
OF GASPARD
DE LA
NUIT.

OLD PARIS

TWO JEWS

I.

Old couples,
Old jealous ones,
Draw all
The bolts.
    Old Song.

TWO JEWS

Two Jews, who had stopped below my window, counted surreptitiously on their fingertips the night's long, drawn-out hours.

"Do you have the money, Rabbi?" the younger asked the older. — "This purse," responded the other, "does it jingle like a small, round bell, doesn't it?"

*

But, then, a bunch of people burst from the neighborhood hovels with a racket. Their cries showered on my windowpanes like shot from a pea-shooter.

They were merely a bunch of the sorriest jokers dashing in high spirits towards the marketplace from where the wind drove up sparks from straw and the smell of something burning.

"Hey! Hey! Lanturelu!" — "My regards to Madame the moon!" — "Hey! Right over here, the Devil's cowl! Two Jews out after curfew!" — "Let's get 'em! Beat the hell out of 'em! Jews by day, curfew-breakers by night!"

*

And cracked bells rang from up above, in Gothic St. Eustache's steeples: — "You ding-dong, ding-dong, sleep, then, ding-dong!"

To M. Louis Boulanger, painter.

NIGHT TRAMPS

II.

I endure
freezure
very sure.
Song of a poor devil.

NIGHT TRAMPS

"Hey! Make room so I can warm myself!" — "That's the last straw! Hogging the fire! This bastard has legs like a vise!"

"One o'clock!" — "It's pitch black out there!" — "Do you know, my fine wood owls, what makes the moon so bright?" — "No!" — "The cuckold's horns that burn there."

"The red embers are scorching the meat!" — "Look how the flame dances blue about the coals! Hey! Which horn-dog beat his horn-bitch?"

"My nose is frozen." — "My shanks are roasted!" — "Do you see anything in the fire, Choupille?" — "Yes. A halberd." — "And you, Grizzly-John?" — "An eye."

"Move over and make room for M. de la Chousserie!" — "There you are, Mister Prosecutor. My, you are warmly furred and gloved for the winter!" — "Yes, indeed! Tom-cats don't get chillblains!"

"Ah! And here are the gentlemen of the watch!" — "Your boots are steaming." — "And the purse snatchers?" — "We killed two of them with our arquebuses. The others escaped across the river."

*

And so it happened that an attorney of the highest court, who frequented places of ill-repute, and those miles gloriosos of the watch, who laughingly recounted the exploits of their wayward arquebus shots, found themselves drawn to a bonfire and the company of some night tramps.

LANTERN

III.

Mummer: "It's dark out; lend me your lantern."
Mercurio: "Bah! Cats have two eyes for lanterns."
A Night at the Carnival.

LANTERN

Alas! Why did I, a little gutter sprite, think there was room, this evening, to snuggle up out of the storm in Madame de Gourgouran's lantern!

I laughed when I heard another sprite getting soaked in the downpour, buzzing around the luminous house, without being able to find the opening through which I had entered. Hah!

Vainly he begged me, hoarse and shivering, to let him at least relight his twisted taper from my candle so he could try to find his way.

Suddenly the yellow paper of the lantern ignited, sparked by a gust of wind that made the signboards hanging like flags along the street creak and groan.

"Jesus, mercy!" a nun cried out, crossing herself with her five fingers. — "May the Devil give you some pokes with a red-hot iron, witch," I cried, spitting more sparks than a firework serpent.

Alas! I, who, up to this morning, could be compared in charms and finery to the goldfinch of that young squire from Luynes. A goldfinch colored scarlet behind the ears.

NESLE TOWER

IV.

At the Nesle Tower there was a guardhouse wherein the watch lodged during the night.
BRANTÔME.

NESLE TOWER

"Jack of clubs!" — "Queen of spades! I win!" — And the old soldier who had lost slammed his fist against the table, sending the pot of winnings all over the floor.

But, then, Master Hugues, the provost, spat into the iron brazier, screwing up his face like a sinner who swallowed a spider while eating his soup.

"Faugh! Are the pork-butchers scalding their hogs at midnight? Good God, there's a straw boat burning on the Seine!"

*

The fire, which was, at first, only a harmless sprite lost in the river mist, soon became a demon on all fours throwing cannon-shot and powerful arquebusades riding a jet of water.

A numberless crowd of jokers, cripples and night tramps rushed over to the river bank and danced jigs before the spiral of flame and smoke.

And Nesle Tower, from which the night watch had exited, weapons on their shoulders, and the tower of the Louvre, from which, through a window, the king and queen saw everything without being seen, both of these towers facing each other glowed red.

A REFINED PERSON

V.

« 61 »

A cock-of-the-walk, a dandy.
Poetry from SCARRON.

A REFINED PERSON

"My fangs sharpened to a point resemble a dragon's tail. My linen is as white as a tablecloth, and my doublet's no older than the crown tapestries.

"Could anyone ever imagine, getting a look at my natty, slouched gait, that hunger, lodged in my belly, tightens there — oh, the pain! — a noose that strangles me as if I were a hanged man!

"Alas! If, from that window where a light flickers, only a roasted lark had fallen onto the corner of my felt hat instead of this faded flower."

"The royal square, this evening, is lit up bright as a chapel with all these huge lanterns!" — "Make way for the litter!" — "Fresh lemonade." — "Macarons from Naples." — "Well now, little fellow, I'll dip my finger into your trout à la sauce! Funny! Where are the spices? Is this some kind of joke?"

"Isn't that Marion de l'Orme in the arms of the Duke de Longueville? Three toy poodles follow her, yapping. — The young courtesan has beautiful diamonds in her eyes! — The old courtier has beautiful rubies about his nose!"

*

And the dandy strutted about, one fist akimbo, elbowing and smiling at passersby. He couldn't afford dinner with what little he had. Instead, he bought a bouquet of violets.

EVENING PRAYERS

VI.

When, near Easter or Christmas, the church, at nightfall,
Filled with muffled steps and burning wax.
      Victor Hugo. *Songs of Twilight.*

Dixit dominus domino meo: Sede a dextris meis.
      Vespers Prayer.

« 66 »

EVENING PRAYERS

Thirty monks, leafing page by page through their psalters as filthy as their beards, praised God, and rained abuse upon the Devil.

*

"Madame, your shoulders are tufts of lilies and roses." — And as the cavalier bowed, the tip of his sword put out one of his valet's eyes.

"Twit," she smirked, "are you making a game of distracting me?" — "Is that *The Imitation of Jesus* that you're reading, Madame?" — "No, it's *The Casino of Love and Gallantry*."

But the service had been recited. She closed her book and rose from her seat. — "Let's get out of here," she said, "I've prayed enough for today!"

*

And I, a pilgrim kneeling down alone beneath the organ pipes, I seemed to hear angels melodiously descend from the heavens.

From afar, I gathered some fragrances coming from the censer, and God permitted that, after that abundant harvest, I reap for the poor a single clutch of flowers.

SERENADE

VII.

At night, all cats are grey.
Old Proverb.

SERENADE

A lute, a guitar and an oboe. Dissonant and ridiculous symphony. Madame Laure at her balcony, behind the jalousie. No lanterns on the road, no lights in the windows. A crescent moon.

*

"Is that you, d'Espignac?" — "Alas! No." — "Is it you, then, my little Almond Blossom?" — "Neither the one nor the other." — "What, you again, M. de la Tournelle? Good evening! Looking for trouble?"

MUSICIANS IN CAPES. — "Master counselor will only get a cold from this, that's all." — "But doesn't this lover fear her husband?" — "Pah! Her husband's in the Indies."

Yet, what was it they were whispering between them? — "A hundred louis a month." — "Charming!" — "A carriage with two heyducks." — "Splendid!" — "A mansion in the princes' quarter." — "Excellent!" — "And my heart, jam-packed with love." — "Oh, pretty slippers for my feet!"

MUSICIANS STILL IN CAPES. — "I hear Madame Laure laugh." — "The cruel bitch is softening." — "Yes, indeed! The art of Orpheus soothed tigers in antiquity!"

MADAME LAURE. — "Come nearer, my darling, so I can slip you my key tied up in a ribbon!" — And master counselor's wig got wet from a dew the stars did not distill. — "Hey! Gueudespin!" shouted the malicious female, retreating from the balcony, "Get me a whip, and run quickly and dry off the gentleman!"

SIR JOHN

VIII.

A solemn person whose gold chain and white sceptre proclaimed authority.

WALTER SCOTT. *The Abbot.* ch. IV.

SIR JOHN

"Sir John," the Queen said to him, "go to the palace courtyard and find out why those two greyhounds are fighting." — And off he went.

And while he was there, the seneschal scolded very harshly the two greyhounds who had been quarreling over a ham bone.

But those two there, snapping at his black breeches and nipping his red stockings, knocked him over easier than if he were a gouty man on crutches.

"Stop! Stop! Help!" — And the guards at the gate rushed over, but those two lean ones' muzzles had already rummaged through the good man's dainty purse.

Meanwhile, the Queen fainted from laughing so hard as she watched from her window in her long, Mechlin lace stomacher, which was as stiff and pleated as a fan.

"And why were they fighting, sir?" — "They were fighting, Madame, because one maintained that you are the most beautiful, the wisest, noblest princess in the universe and the other did not."

To M. Sainte-Beuve.

MIDNIGHT MASS

IX.

Christus natus est nobis; venitus, adoremus.
Birth of Our Lord J. C.

We have neither fire nor home,
Give us the part after life now.
Old Song.

MIDNIGHT MASS

The good Lady and the noble Lord de Chateauvieux were breaking evening bread, and the chaplain was blessing the food, when they happened to hear the shuffling of wooden clogs at the door. It was a group of small children singing a Christmas carol.

"Good Lady de Chateauvieux, hurry up! Everyone's already on their way to the church. Hurry up, before the taper burning above your prie-dieu, in the Chapel of the Angels, dies out and wax drops like little stars on your vellum prayer books and on your small square seat cushion! — Listen, it's the first peal of bells for midnight mass!

"Noble Lord de Chateauvieux, hurry up, before the Lord de Grugel, who's just passing by over there with his paper lantern, grabs in your absence the place of honor in the pew with the brothers of St. Antoine. — Listen, it's the second peal of the bells for midnight mass!

"Chaplain, hurry up! The organ pipes are rumbling and the canons have begun reciting. Hurry up! The faithful are assembled, and you're still at table! — Listen, it's the third peal of the bells for midnight mass!"

The small children blew on their fingers, but were not chilled long waiting. And on the Gothic threshold, white with snow, the chaplain treated each of them, in the name of the masters of the house, to a waffle and a copper coin.

*

Meanwhile, no further bell rang. The good Lady plunged her hands up to her elbows into a muff, the noble Lord covered his ears with a mortier, and the humble priest, his head wrapped in an amice, walked behind them, his missal tucked under an arm.

BIBLIOPHILE

X.

« 81 »

An Elzevir made his nerves tingle; but what plunged him into an ecstatic rapture, that was an Henri Etienne.
Biography of Martin Spickler.

BIBLIOPHILE

It was not some painting from the Flemish school, a David Téniers, or a Breughel d'Enfer, a picture so smoky you cannot even see the Devil there.

It was a manuscript gnawed by rats along its edges, written in a thoroughly jumbled handwriting and penned in blue and red ink.

"I suspect the author," said the bibliophile, "to have lived at the end of Louis the XII's reign; the king who, in our memory, was magnanimous and paternal."

"Yes," he continued with a solemn and pensive air, "yes, he'd have been a cleric, in the House of Chateauvieux."

Now he consults a mammoth folio entitled, *The Directory of French Nobility*, in which he found only the House of Chateauneuf mentioned.

"Never mind," he said, taken a little aback, "Chateauneuf and Chateauvieux merely amount to the same chateau. Anyways, it's about time to rename the Pont-Neuf."

HERE ENDS THE SECOND
BOOK OF THE FANTASIES
OF GASPARD
DE LA
NUIT.

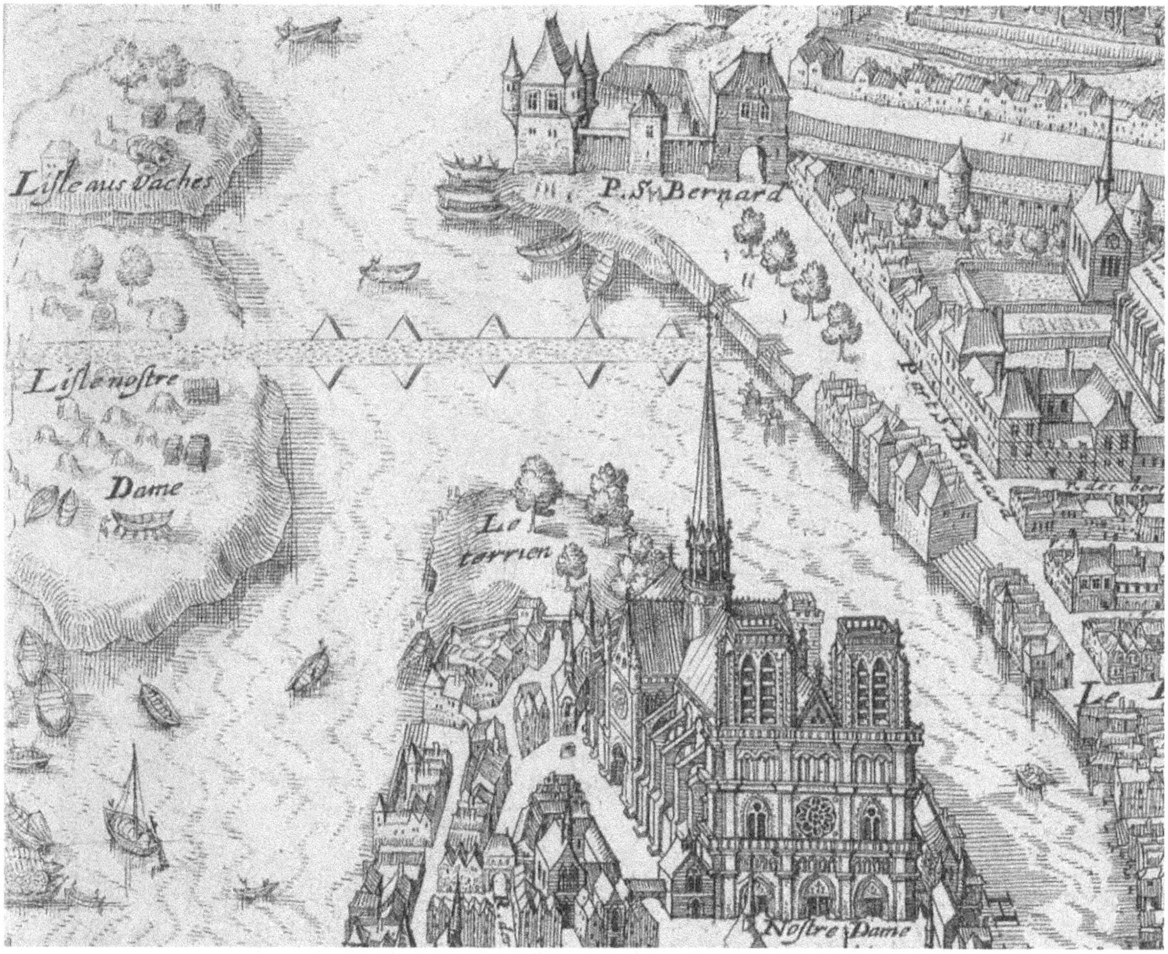

HERE BEGINS THE THIRD
BOOK OF THE FANTASIES
OF GASPARD
DE LA
NUIT.

NIGHT AND ITS SPELLS

GOTHIC CHAMBER

I.

Nox et solitudo plenae sunt diabolo.
FATHERS OF THE CHURCH.
Night, my room is full of demons.

GOTHIC CHAMBER

"Oh, the earth's a scented flower whose pistil and stamens are the moon and stars!" I whispered to the night.

And eyes heavy with sleep, I closed my window. Its grillework outlined the cross of Calvary, black against the yellow glow from the stained glass.

*

And yet — if it were only, on this midnight, that hour emblazoned with dragons and demons, if it were only some gnome downing my lamp-oil again!

If it were only some wet nurse rocking a small, stillborn baby in my father's breastplate, droning a lullaby.

If it were only the skeleton of a foot-soldier imprisoned behind the wall, knocking against the wainscotting with his forehead, elbows and knees.

If it were only my grandfather coming downstairs with his body all maggot-eaten, dipping his gauntlet into the font's holy water.

But, no, it's Scarbo who's gnawing my neck. And now he plunges his iron finger glowing red from the stove into my bleeding wound — such loving cautery!

SCARBO

II.

Dear Lord, grant me at the hour of my death the last rights, a linen shroud, a fir coffin and a dry place for my grave.
Paternosters of a General.

SCARBO

Scarbo muttered much into my ear that night: — "Whether you die absolved or damned, you'll have a cobweb for a shroud. And, don't worry, I'll wind the spider in it with you."

By the time I answered him my eyes were red from having cried so much. — "Oh, may I at least have an aspen leaf for a shroud so I can be lulled by lake breezes?"

"No!" the snickering dwarf jeered. — "You're going to be fodder for dung-beetles hunting down gnats blinded by the setting sun."

"How about," I asked him with my cheeks still streaming with tears, "how about if I were sucked up by a tarantula with an elephant-size trunk? Would you like that better?"

"That'd be good," he added. — "But console yourself with the fact that you'll have a snakeskin with its thin, gold-flecked bands for a shroud. I'll wrap you in it tighter than a mummy.

"And in St. Bénigne's filthy crypt I'll lay you to rest propped up against a wall. There you'll hear at your leisure small babies crying in Limbo."

MADMAN

III.

A copper, or better yet,
If you'd prefer, a gold doubloon.
Manuscript from the King's Library.

MADMAN

When the moon combed her hair with a large-toothed ebony comb a shower of glow-worms plated the hills, meadows and woods with silver.

While my weathervane screeched in the wind, Scarbo, that gnome with boundless wealth, winnowed ducats and florins onto my roof. They jumped and flitted about the rooftop melodiously. False notes of pieces were strewn all about the street.

How he sniggered, this madman who wanders every night throughout the deserted city with one eye on the moon and the other — punctured!

"I could care less about the moon," he grumbled as he picked up the Devil's tokens. "I'll buy a pillory and warm myself in the sun in it."

But he couldn't escape the moon, the setting moon. — And so there he is now, that Scarbo, secretly minting ducats and florins in my cellar. I can hear him pounding his hammer.

Meanwhile, with its two little horns in front, a snail that had strayed in the night inched its way across my illuminated windowpanes.

DWARF

IV.

—"You! Get on a horse!"
—"Eh? Why not? I've often gone galloping on one of the Laird of Lulithgow's greyhounds!"
  Scottish ballad.

DWARF

I caught this furtive butterfly as I sat in my chair. It came from the shadow thrown by my curtains and must have hatched from a moonbeam or maybe from a dew drop.

The fluttering phalaena tried to extricate its wings that I held captive between my fingers, and rewarded me with a ransom of perfumes.

Suddenly the wandering little creature flew away. But — O horror! — it left in my lap a monstrous and deformed larva with a human face.

"Where's your soul? What else can I ride?" — "My soul, a hack lamed from the day's hauling, rests now on a stable-litter gilt with dreams."

Charged with fright, my soul escaped across the ashen web of twilight, above black horizons notched with Gothic steeples.

But the dwarf, hanging on for dear life in its neighing flight, spun himself like a spindle amid the flaxen tow of its white mane.

MOONLIGHT

V.

Wake up sleepers,
And pray for your sins.
Town-crier's cry.

MOONLIGHT

Oh, how pleasant it is when the hour is struck in the steeple at night, how sweet to gaze at the moon, with her nose looking like a gold coin!

Two lepers wailed beneath my window. A dog howled at the crossroads. A cricket on my hearth chirped his prophecies very softly.

But before long my ear interrogated nothing more than a profound silence. The lepers returned to their huts to the sound of the jack-in-the-clock beating his wife.

The dog threaded its way down a small alley. It passed in front of the night watch's halberds that were covered with rust from the rain and chilled by the north wind.

The cricket fell asleep as soon as the last spark shed its final glimmer among the fireplace ashes.

And as for me — since fever breeds incoherency — it seemed that the moon's face was screwed up and her tongue dangled from her mouth like someone who had just been hung.

To M. Louis Boulanger, painter.

PATROL BENEATH THE BELL

VI.

It was a massive structure, nearly square, surrounded by ruins, and whose principal spire, still possessed of its clockworks, dominated the entire district.
                    FENIMORE COOPER.

PATROL BENEATH THE BELL

A dozen magicians danced below the church of St. Jean's tall steeple. They conjured up one storm after another. Huddled in a corner of my bed, terrified, I counted a dozen voices ceremoniously traversing the darkness.

The moon immediately ran and hid behind some clouds. A rainstorm with lightning and strong gales lashed at my window. Weathervanes shrieked in the wind as cranes kept watch on the downpour in the woods.

The first string of my lute that hung on the wall broke. My goldfinch beat its wings against its cage. Some curious imp turned a page of *The Romance of the Rose* resting on my desk.

But suddenly a great clap of thunder rumbled from above the church. The enchanters fell — all were struck dead. From a distance I saw their magic books burn as if they were torches lighting the dark steeple.

That frightful flash swept together the red flames of purgatory and hell along the walls of the Gothic church. The flames grew higher than the houses below the huge statue of St. Jean.

The weathervanes rusted. The moon dissolved the pearl-grey clouds. The rainfall was reduced to no more than a slow dripping from the eaves. And strong gusts of wind, throwing open my badly shut window, flung on my pillow some jasmine flowers shaken loose by the storm.

DREAM

VII.

I've had so many dreams, but I can never make any sense of them.
Pantagruel, Book III.

DREAM

It was night. There were at first (so I saw, so I say) a monastery with thick, high walls cracked by the moon, a forest thick with winding paths — and Morimont* teeming with capes and hats.

Then there were (so I heard, so I say) a bell's funereal knell answering the mournful sobs coming from a cell — such plaintive wailings and biting laughter from which every leaf among the trees shuddered — and the undertone of prayers of somber penitents accompanying a criminal to his punishment.

There were also (so the dream went, so I say) a dead monk laid down among the ashes of the dying — and a young girl who struggled as she hung from the branches of an oak. — And, finally, the executioner was securing me, already a frightful sight, onto the spokes of the torture wheel.

Brother Augustin, the deceased prior, dressed in his Franciscan's robes, will be accorded the honors of the mortuary chapel. Marguerite, killed by her lover, will be buried in her innocent-white gown and waked surrounded by four beeswax tapers.

But as for me, the executioner shattered his metal bar on the first blow as if it were glass. Torrents of rain quenched the somber penitents' torches. The crowds were swept away by an overflowing and swift stream. — And I continued with other dreams until I woke.

*In Dijon, from time immemorial, the place of executions.

MY GREAT-GRANDFATHER

VIII.

Everything in that chamber remained the same as in the past, except for the tapestries hanging in tatters, and spiders, spinning their webs there among the dust.
WALTER SCOTT. *Woodstock*.

MY GREAT-GRANDFATHER

The venerable figures inhabiting the Gothic tapestry, stirred slightly by the wind, greeted one another — and my great-grandfather stepped into the room despite being dead for the last eighty years!

There! — It's there, right in front of that prie-dieu that the great counselor-at-law knelt. Great-grandpa's beard kissed my yellow missal opened to this very passage with a ribbon bookmark.

He muttered his prayers as long as the night lasted without uncrossing his arms from underneath his violet silk cloak, without casting a glance towards me — his posterity tucked away in his bed, in his very own dusty, canopied bed!

Bones still chilled through with fear, I noticed that his eyes were empty even though he seemed to read. — His lips did not move even though I knew I heard him pray. — His fingers were fleshless even though they sparkled with precious stones.

I wondered whether I was awake or asleep. — I wondered whether this ghastliness was due to the moon or Lucifer — whether it was midnight or daybreak.

ONDINE

IX.

.... I thought I heard
A subtle harmony enchant my sleep,
And near me diffused a murmur equal
To songs interrupted by a sad and tender voice.
        CH. BRUGNOT. *The Two Sylphs*.

ONDINE

"Listen! — Listen! — It's me. It's Ondine scattering these droplets ever so lightly against the clear diamond-shapes of your windowpanes illuminated by dim moonbeams. And over here, in a moire gown, the lady of the manor surveys from her balcony a delightful starry night and a lovely sleeping lake.

"Each wave is a water-sprite floating along the current. Each current is a path that meanders towards my palace. My palace, crafted from water, lies at the bottom of the lake among the triad of fire, earth and air.

"Listen! — Listen! — My father stirs the water with a branch from a budding alder tree. You can hear the frogs croaking. And my sisters caress with their arms of froth and foam isles blooming with grass, water lilies and gladioli. They scoff at the decrepit and bearded willow dipping its leaves into the water as if it were fishing with rod and reel!"

*

Once her song ceased to babble and flow, she begged me to accept her ring and be Ondine's mate. She asked me to visit her palace and become king of the lakes.

I answered her that I was in love with a mortal. Vexed and sulky, she shed some tears, sharply burst out laughing and then vanished into a sudden shower that blossomed white all along my blue windowpanes.

SALAMANDER

X.

He flung into the fire some branches of
sacred holly that crackled as they burned.
CH. NODIER. *Trilby*.

SALAMANDER

"Cricket, my friend, are you dead? You remain deaf to the noise of my hissing. You're blind to my glittering fire."

However affectionate the words of the salamander might have been, the cricket did not make any answer. It may be that the cricket was sleeping a magical sleep. Or perhaps he might have taken a fancy to being taciturn.

"Oh, sing me the song you sing every evening from your tiny lodgings in the ashes and soot, from behind the iron slab decorated with an escutcheon of three heraldic fleurs-de-lys."

The cricket still did not answer. The disconsolate salamander listened hard for the cricket's voice to no avail. Soon the salamander was humming with its flames turning all sorts of colors: rose, blue, red, yellow, white and violet.

"He's dead! My friend the cricket's dead!" he wailed. — I listened to his sighs and sobs until the flames, livid now, diminished in the desolate firebox.

"He's dead! And since he's dead, I want to die!" — The vines had been consumed. The flames crept over the embers, casting their last farewells toward the pot-hook in the fireplace, and the salamander died from starvation.

SABBATH HOUR

XI.

Who passes through this valley at so late an hour?
   H. DE LATOUCHE. *King of the Alders.*

SABBATH HOUR

It's here! Already among the dense thickets where the phosphorescent eyes of a wild cat crouching among the branches are barely discernable —

On the sides of boulders that get drenched during the night, dripping dew and glow-worms from their mossy tresses into chasms —

Along the banks of a rushing stream spraying white foam onto pines and drizzling grey mist onto castle walls —

An innumerable throng gathers that the old woodcutter, slowed on his way along the footpaths by the load of wood on his back, hears but does not see.

From oak to oak, knoll to knoll, a thousand indistinct, doleful, frightful cries speak to him: — "Hmm! Hmm!" — "Hoo! Hoo!" — "Cuckoo! Cuckoo!"

It's here, the gallows! Look, there, in the mist, there's a skinflint searching for something in the moist grass, lit by the golden luster of the glory of an executed man's hand.

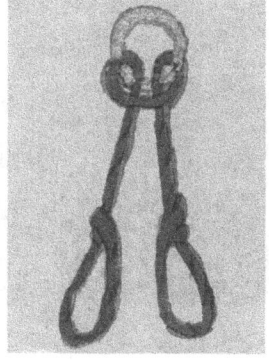

HERE ENDS THE THIRD
BOOK OF THE FANTASIES
OF GASPARD
DE LA
NUIT.

HERE BEGINS THE FOURTH
BOOK OF THE FANTASIES
OF GASPARD
DE LA
NUIT.

CHRONICLES

MASTER OGIER
(1407)
I.

« 137 »

The aforementioned King Charles VI was very easygoing and much loved; and his subjects had but great hatred for the dukes of Orleans and Burgundy, who imposed excessive taxes throughout the kingdom.
The Annals and Chronicles of France, from the Trojan War to King Louis XI, by MASTER NICOLLE GILES.

MASTER OGIER

"Sire," Master Ogier asked the king, who was looking through a tiny window in his chapel at old Paris brightened by a ray of sun, "don't you hear that commotion in the courtyard of your Louvre from these greedy sparrows chattering through this leafy net of vines?"

"Yes, indeed!" replied the king, "it's a very entertaining racket."

"These vines are in your courtyard, yet you won't profit from their harvest," countered Master Ogier with an innocent smile. "Sparrows are brazen thieves, and they like to peck so much, they will always be peckers. They'll harvest your vineyard for you."

"Oh! Nay, my friend! I will chase them away," cried the king!

Then he brought to his lips an ivory whistle that hung from a link on his gold chain, and drew from it such shrill and piercing sounds that the sparrows flew into the highest nooks and crannies of the palace.

"Sire," Master Ogier then said, "allow me to draw a parable from this. These sparrows are your nobles and these vines are your people. Some feast at the expense of the other. Sire, who steals from the lowest, also steals from the highest. Enough looting! Blow your whistle, and harvest your own vineyard."

Master Ogier rubbed the point of his cap between his fingers nervously. Charles VI sadly shook his head, and then taking the hand of the Paris burger, he sighed: — "You're too much a sensible man!"

LOUVRE PRIVATE ENTRANCE

II.

The dwarf was lazy, unpredictable and detestable, but he was loyal and his service agreeable to his master.

WALTER SCOTT. *The Lay of the Minstrel.*

LOUVRE PRIVATE ENTRANCE

That little light crossed the frozen Seine below the Nesle Tower, and now was no more than a hundred paces away, bobbing and swaying in the fog, inducing such infernal and prodigious fear by emitting a cackle like some mocking laugh!

"Who's there?" shouted the Swiss guard at the sentry-box next to the Louvre's private entrance.

The little light quickened its approach but did not hasten to answer. Soon a drawf's figure appeared dressed in a tunic with gold sequins and wearing a cap with a silver bell, from whose hand dangled a red candle glowing within a lantern's diamond panes.

"Who's there?" repeated the Swiss guard, in a trembling voice, positioning his arquebus against his cheek.

The dwarf snuffed the candle in his lantern, and the arquebusier could make out his wizened and emaciated features, and his eyes shone with evil, and his white beard was heavy with frost.

"Hey! hey! Friend, be careful not to fire your arquebus. There, there! Holy shit! By the blood of God! You exhale only death and bloodshed!" cried the dwarf with a voice no less quivering than that of the montagnard.

"Friend yourself! Jeez! But, again, who are you?" asked the Swiss guard a little bit reassured. — And he replaced the fuse for his arquebus on his metal helmet.

"My father is King Nacbuc and my mother is Queen Nacbuca. Yip! Yip! Yahoo!" replied the dwarf, sticking his tongue way out and pirouetting twice on one foot.

That response got the soldier's teeth chattering. Fortunately, he remembered that he had a rosary hanging from his wisent hide belt.

"If your father is King Nacbuc, *pater noster*, and your mother is Queen Nacbuca, *qui es in coelis*, doesn't that make you the Devil, *sanctificetur nomen tuum*?" he stammered, scared shitless.

"What? No!" said the lantern holder. "I'm my Lord the King's dwarf who arrives this evening from Compiègne, and I'm his advance party to make ready his entry through the Louvre's private entrance. The password is: 'Dame Anne de Bretagne and St. Aubin du Cormier.'"

THE FLEMISH

III.

The Flemish, a defiant and stubborn people.
Memoirs of Olivier de la Marche.

THE FLEMISH

The battle had been raging since Nones, when those from Bruges broke and abruptly turned aboutface. There was, on one hand, so much confusion, and on the other, such unrelenting pursuit, that when crossing a bridge a good number of rebels tumbled headlong into the river — men, banners, wagons.

The count entered Bruges the next day with a marvelous cohort of knights. His heralds who preceded him blew their trumpets ever so formidably. Some looters, daggers in hand, ran about here and there, and ahead of them fled our terrified pigs.

The neighing cavalcade headed towards city hall. There the burgomaster and the aldermen begged for mercy on their knees, their mantels and hoods scraping the ground. But the count had sworn, with two fingers on the Bible, to slaughter the red boar in its lair.

"My lord!"

"Burn the city!"

"My lord!"

"Hang them all!"

They only set fire to a poor neighborhood on the outskirts of the city. Only captains of the militia hung from the gallows, and the red boar was removed from our flags. Bruges had saved itself by a hundred thousand gold crowns.

THE HUNT
(1412)
IV.

Let's go! Let the stag run a bit,
he said to him.
 Unpublished poetry.

THE HUNT

And the hunt went on and on, the day being exceptionally fine, over mountains and valleys, through fields and woods, with varlets running, trumpets blaring, hounds baying, hawks reconnoitering, and two cousins riding side by side, and taking down stags and wild boars in the undergrowth with their spears, and herons and storks in the air with their crossbows.

"Cousin," said Hubert to Regnault, "it seems to me that you aren't looking too happy, even though we made peace this morning. What gives?"

"I'm fine!" was the answer to him.

Regnault had the red eye of a madman or someone who's cursed. Hubert seemed somewhat unconvinced, but the hunt continued, went on and on, the day being exceptionally fine, through mountains and valleys, through fields and woods.

But suddenly a troop of footmen, laying ambush in a grotto inhabited by fairies, rushed out, spears lowered, against the carefree hunt. Regnault unsheathed his sword, and it was — cross yourself! — to hack several blows through the body of his cousin who dropped from his stirrups.

"Die, die!" cried the traitor.

"Our Lady! Have pity!" — and the hunt stopped, even though the day was exceptionally fine, through mountains and valleys, through fields and woods.

The soul of Hubert, Sire of Maugiron, appeared before God, mercilessly murdered on the third of July, year fourteen hundred and twelve; and may the Devil take the soul of Regnault, Lord of Aubépine, his cousin and murderer! Amen.

BLACK RIDERS

V.

« 153 »

Once upon a time Hilarion was tempted by a female demon who gave him a cup of wine and flowers.
Lives of the Desert Fathers.

BLACK RIDERS

Three black riders, each accompanied on their saddles by a gypsy, were trying at midnight to enter a monastery via a trick of some sort.

"Hey! hey!"

It was one of them standing on his stirrups.

"Hey! Give us shelter against the storm! Why are you mistrustful? Take a look through the peep hole. These cuties lashed with us, these casks slung over our shoulders, aren't they fifteen-year-old girls and wine to drink?"

The monastery seemed to be asleep.

"Hey! hey!"

One of the gypsies shivered with cold.

"Hey! Give us shelter, in the name of the blessed mother of the Savior! We're lost pilgrims. The glass of our reliquaries, the edge of our hoods, the folds of our coats drip with rain, and our steeds, who stumble with fatigue, have lost their shoes on the road."

A light radiated from a door crack.

"Back, demons of the night!"

They were the prior and his monks in a procession armed with candles.

"Avast ye, lying daughters! God watch over us, if you are flesh and blood, and if you are not ghosts, from hosting in our courtyard heathens or at least heretics!"

"Let's go! Let's go!" cried the dark horsemen. — "Let's get out of here! Let's get away!" — And the sound of their horses galloping off into the distance was swept away on the wind whistling through river and forest.

"What gives with rebuffing thus fifteen-year-old sinners who we would have brought about penance!" grumbled a young monk as blond and adorable as a cherub.

"Brother!" whispered the abbot into the hollow of the monk's ear, "you forget that Madame Aliénor and her niece are waiting for us upstairs to confess them."

ILLUSTRIOUS DETACHMENTS
(1364)
VI.

Urbem ingredientur, per muros current, domos conscendent,
per fenestras intrabunt quasi fur.
     THE PROPHET JOEL, *Chap. II, v. 9.*

ILLUSTRIOUS DETACHMENTS

I

A few raiders, lost in the woods, warmed themselves over a watch fire, around which thickets, darkness and ghosts abounded.

"Here's some news!" said a crossbowman. "King Charles V dispatches my Lord Bertrand du Guesclin to us with promises of support. However, one does not snag the Devil like a blackbird in a net trap."

The whole group roared with laughter as one, and this savage gaiety redoubled again when a bagpipe losing its swelling whimpered like a teething brat.

"What the fuck?" finally replied an archer, "Aren't you bored with this idle life? Have you pillaged enough castles, monasteries? I'm neither drunk nor full. Curses on Jacques d'Arquiel, our captain! — The wolf's now no more than a greyhound pup. — And long live Master Bertrand du Guesclin, if he pays me well enough and sends me off to battle!"

Now flames from the embers glowed red and blue, and the faces of the rogue men blued and reddened. From a nearby farm a rooster crowed.

"The rooster crowed and St. Peter denied Our Lord!" murmured a crossbowman as he crossed himself.

II

"A godsend! — We hit the jackpot! It's raining coins!"

"I'll shower each of you with a bushelful."

"Are you pulling my leg?"

"Knight's honor!"

"And who's going to give you — yes, you — such a huge fortune?"

"Fighting."

"Where?"

"In Spain. There, disbelievers throw gold around with shovels, and they shoe their palfreys with gold. Does a journey there agree with you? We'll hunt down Moors, those Philistines, and ransom them!"

"Spain's far away, sir!"

"You've got soles on your shoes."

"That's not enough."

"The king's treasurers will pay you an advance of a hundred thousand florins. That might put some fire in your belly."

"Done! We'll drape the fleurs-de-lys of your banner on the thorny branch of our Burgundian helmets. How does that ballad go?"

> "Oh! on the road
> The gay mercenary!"

"Ah, yes! Are your tents struck? Are your mule carriers loaded? Let's get a move on. — Yes, my fellow soldiers of fortune, plant an acorn here when you leave, and when you return it will be a towering oak!"

And one could hear the packs of Jacques d'Arquiel barking, chasing a stag partway up a hill.

« 162 »

III

The marauders marched, heading off in waves, hackbuts on their shoulders. An archer in the rear was arguing with a Jew.

The archer held up three fingers.

The Jew held up two.

The archer spat in his face.

The Jew wiped his beard.

The archer held up three fingers.

The Jew held up two.

The archer let loose a slap on him.

The Jew held up three fingers.

"Thief! You wanted two gold coins for this doublet," shouted the archer.

"Have mercy! Here's three," cried the Jew.

It was a magnificent velvet doublet brocaded with a silver hunting horn on each sleeve. It bore a hole and blood stains on it.

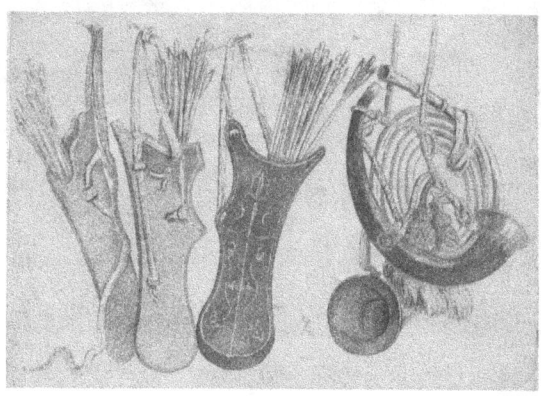

To M. P. J. David, sculptor.

LEPERS

VII.

Do not approach these places
They're the leper's lairs.
The Leper's Lay.

LEPERS

Each morning, as soon as the branches had drunk the dew, the door of the lepers' colony swung open on its hinges, and the lepers, much like ancient anchorites, disappeared all day long into the wilderness — Adamite valleys, primitive paradises whose distant, tranquil green and wooded scapes are populated only by does grazing on the flower-strewn grass, and herons fishing in clear marshes.

Some worked in their small gardens: a rose was more fragrant to them, a fig tastier, if cultivated by their own hand. A few others wove wicker traps or carved boxwood cups in stone caves with a bed of sand layered by a gushing spring and carpeted with an overgrowth of bindweed. This is how they sought to stave off time that passed so quickly for joy, so slowly for suffering!

But there were some who no longer even bothered to cross the threshold of the colony. Those weary, languishing, sad folk, who had been marked with the cross of disease without cure, their shadows paced between the four walls of the cloister, high and whitewashed, with an eye on the sundial whose needle hastened the exhaustion of their lives and the approach of eternity.

And when they leaned against the thick columns, they became lost in themselves, nothing interrupting the silence of this cloister except the cries of a triad of storks plowing through the clouds, except for a monk telling the beads of his rosary as he walked down a corridor, and except for the rale of the watchman's rattle every evening who led these gloomy recluses from the dining hall back to their cells.

TO A BIBLIOPHILE

VIII.

My children, there are no more knights than those in books.
Stories told by a grandmother to her grandchildren.

TO A BIBLIOPHILE

Why retell the maggot-infested and sordid tales of the Middle Ages, when chivalry has long ago vanished, along with its bards' songs, along with the enchantments of its fairies and the glorious deeds of its valiant knights?

What do our marvelous legends matter to our cynical century? St. Georges breaking a lance against Charles VII at the tournament at Luçon, the Holy Spirit descending in full view of the assembled Council of Trent, and the Wandering Jew who waylaid Bishop Gotzelin near the city of Langres to tell him about Our Lord's passion.

Nowadays the three disciplines proper to knights are disparaged. No one's curious any longer to learn at what age one hoods a gyrfalcon, how a bastard displays his coat of arms, and when at night Mars comes into conjunction with Venus.

Every tradition of war and love is forgotten, and I hope even my tales will not share the same fate as Geneviève de Brabant's lament, whose peddler of her likenesses no longer knows how her story started and has no idea how it ends!

HERE ENDS THE FOURTH
BOOK OF FANTASIES
OF GASPARD
DE LA
NUIT.

HERE BEGINS THE FIFTH
BOOK OF FANTASIES
OF GASPARD
DE LA
NUIT.

SPAIN AND ITALY

THE CELL

I.

Spain, classic country of imbroglios, knifings, serenades and auto-da-fés!
Excerpt from a literary review.

.... And I won't hear anymore
The locks that close on the eternal recluse.
ALFRED DE VIGNY. *Prison.*

THE CELL

Down below, tonsured monks walk, silent and meditative, rosaries in hand, and slowly measure from column to column, tomb to tomb, the cobblestone paths of the cloister, accompanied by the tap-tap of a faint echo.

You there, is this how you pass the time, young recluse, alone in your cell, amusing yourself by drawing obscene figures on the blank pages of your prayer book, and rouging with a scandalous ochre the bony cheeks of that skull?

He hasn't forgotten, this young recluse, that his mother's a gypsy, that his father's *the* thief among thieves; and he'd prefer to hear, at the break of day, the trumpet sound the saddle call to mount his horse than the bell tolling matins to scurry off to church!

He hasn't forgotten that he danced the bolero below the towering cliffs of the Sierras in Granada with a brunette wearing silver earrings, and who played ivory castanets; and he'd rather make love in a gypsy camp than pray to God in a monastery.

A ladder has been secretly braided from the straw of his pallet; two bars have been noiselessly sawn with a dull file. The distance from the convent to the Sierras in Granada is less than the distance from hell to paradise!

Once night has shut everyone's eyes, put all doubt to bed, the young recluse will relight his lamp and step out of his cell, inching along, with a blunderbuss thrust under his robe.

MULE DRIVERS

II.

This guy only interrupts his endless tale to urge on his mules by giving them the names of *beautiful* and *valiant,* or to scold them by calling them *lazy* and *stubborn.*
CHATEAUBRIAND. *The Last Abencerage.*

MULE DRIVERS

These dark Andalusians tell their rosaries or braid their hair, unswayed by the lulling rock of their mules' gait. Some of these mule drivers sing the hymn of the pilgrims of St. Jacques, something that is repeated throughout a hundred caves in the Sierras. Others fire their rifles at the sun.

"Here's the place," said one of the guides, "where we buried José Matéos last week, killed by a bullet to the back of his neck in an attack by robbers. The grave has been dug up, and the body gone."

"The body's not far," said one of the mule drivers, "I see it floating at the bottom of the ravine, swollen with water like a goatskin."

"Our Lady of Atocha, protect us!" cried the dark Andalusians, unswayed by the lulling rock of their mules' gait.

"What's that hut at the crest of that rise?" asked a nobleman through a window in his sedan chair. — "Is that the loggers' hut who have cast into the torrent's raging chasm these massive tree trunks, or that of the shepherds who graze their starved goats on these barren slopes?"

"It is," replied one mule driver, "the cell of an old hermit who was found dead this fall on his bed of leaves. There was a rope wound tight around his neck, and his tongue was hanging out of his mouth."

"Our Lady of Atocha, protect us!" cried the dark Andalusians, unswayed by the lulling rock of their mules' gait.

"Those three horsemen, who were hiding behind their cloaks, watched us like hawks as they passed near us. They are not with us. Who are they?" asked a monk with a filthy beard and robe.

"If they aren't," replied another mule driver, "constables from the village of Cienfugos on rounds, then they are thieves sent ahead to reconnoiter by their leader, the infernal Gil Pueblo."

"Our Lady of Atocha, protect us!" cried the dark Andalusians, unswayed by the lulling rock of their mules' gait.

"Did you hear that blunderbuss shot that went off up there in the scrub?" asked an ink merchant, so poor that he walked barefoot. "Look! The smoke dissolves into the air!"

"Those are," replied a mule driver, "our people who are scouring the bushes round here. They set off rounds to scare away brigands. Ladies and gentlemen, courage, and spur your steeds onward."

"Our Lady of Atocha, protect us!" cried the dark Andalusians, unswayed by the lulling rock of their mules' gait.

And all the travelers took off at a gallop accompanied by a huge cloud of dust lit by the sun. Mules threaded their way among immense granite boulders, the torrent roared in roiling eddies, the forests filled with such troublesome noises. And from the deepest solitude there issued indistinctly threatening voices stirred up by the wind. Those voices sometimes drew near, sometimes moved away, as if a gang of thieves lurked about.

MARQUIS D'AROCA

III.

Embark on the grand highway of thievery, you will earn your keep.
CALDERÓN.

MARQUIS D'AROCA

Who doesn't like, during the dog days, a bed of moss and leaves on an oak's shady side in the woods, when screeching jays compete for shade and a perch?

*

Two thieves yawned, asking what time it was from the gypsy who woke them by prodding them like pigs with his foot.

"Get up!" barked the guy. "Get up! It's time to get moving. The Marquis d'Aroca and his six deputies are picking up the scent of our trail."

"Who's that? Is it the Marquis d'Aroca whose timepiece I swiped during the procession of the Reverend Dominican Fathers of Santillane?" posited one of the thieves.

"The Marquis d'Aroca whose mule I rustled at the Salamanca fair!" added the other.

"The man himself," snapped the gypsy. "Let's get a move on so we can reach the Trappists where we can hide for a novena wearing their robes!"

"Stop! Hold on! First give me back my watch and my mule!"

It was the Marquis d'Aroca, leading his six deputies. With one hand he parted the pale light leaves of some hazelnut trees, and with the other pointed the tip of his sword at the thieves.

HENRIQUEZ

IV.

I can see it clearly; it's my destiny to be hung or married.
LOPE DE VEGA.

HENRIQUEZ

"I've commanded you for a year," their leader said to his men, "but someone else will be taking over. I'm going to marry a rich widow from Cordoba, and I renounce my bandit's stiletto for the magistrate's straight and narrow."

He opened a chest: it was the booty that was to be divvied up — a jumble of sacred vessels, jewels, heavy coins, a shower of pearls, and a river of diamonds.

"For you, Henriquez, some earrings and the Marquis d'Aroca's ring! Especially for you, who killed him with a rifle shot in his sedan chair!"

Henriquez slid the bloody topaz onto his finger, and hung from his ears amethysts cut in the shape of blood drops.

Such was the fate of those earrings with which the Duchess of Medina-Coeli had adorned herself, and which Henriquez, a month later, gave in exchange for a kiss from the prison jailer's daughter!

Such was the fate of that ring a nobleman purchased from an emir for the price of a white mare, and for which Henriquez paid for a glass of brandy, just a few minutes before being hung!

THE ALARM

V.

Never parting from his rifle more than Dona Inès from the ring of her beloved!

Spanish song.

THE ALARM

La Posada,* with a peacock on its roof, with its windows and its approach path winding up the mountainside illuminated by the distant fire of the setting sun.

"Shhh! Do any of you hear something?" asked one of the outlaws, pressing his ear against a crack in the shutter.

"My mule," replied one mule driver, "farted in the stable."

"Asshole!" cried another bandit. "I cocked this rifle because of a mule fart? Alarm! alarm! A trumpet! Here come the dragoons decked in yellow!"

Amid the clatter of pots, the strumming of a guitar, servants' laughter, the noise of the crowd, suddenly a silence descended through which the buzzing flight of a fly could be heard.

But it was only a cowherd's horn. The mule drivers, before bridling their mules in order to decamp, drained their half-drunk wineskins. And the bandits who groped in vain the fat ugly lasses of the dark inn, climbed up to their garret rooms, yawning with boredom, fatigue and sleepiness.

* A small Spanish inn.

PADRE PUGNACCIO

VI.

Rome is a city where there are more cops than townspeople, more monks than cops.
Journey to Italy.

He who laughs last laughs best.
Popular proverb.

PADRE PUGNACCIO

Padre Pugnaccio, cranium poking from his hood, climbed the stairs of St. Peter's dome, sandwiched between two worshippers wrapped in mantillas. One could hear the bells as well as angels quarreling in the clouds.

One of the worshippers — it was the aunt — recited an ave for every bead on her rosary; and the other — it was her niece — was casting sidelong glances at a handsome officer of the Pope's Guards.

The monk muttered to the old woman: "Please make a donation to my monastery." — While the officer slipped the young girl a musk-scented love note.

The sinner wiped away a few tears, the ingenue blushed with requited attraction, the monk calculated the yield of a thousand piastres at twelve percent interest, and the officer twirled the tips of his mustache in a pocket mirror.

And the Devil, hiding in Padre Pugnaccio's enormous sleeve, sneered like Punchinello!

MASKED CANTO

VII.

Venice with a masked face.
LORD BYRON.

MASKED CANTO

It's not with a monk's robe and rosary, it's with the tambourine and fool's habit that I, myself, alive, undertake this pilgrimage unto death!

Our noisy group ran to St. Mark's Square from Master Arlecchino's inn, who had invited us all to a feast of macaroni with olive oil and polenta with garlic.

Let's join hands, ephemeral monarch, you who are capped with a gilt paper crown, and you all, his freakish subjects, who form his retinue with your coats patched with a thousand rags, with your scraggly tallow beards and your wooden swords.

Let's join hands to sing and dance a roundelay, unnoticed by our inquisitor, under the magical splendor of this evening's firewheels roaring like daylight.

Let's sing and dance, we who are joyful, while those who are melancholy wend down the canal on the gondoliers' benches, and weep while gazing up at the stars.

Let's dance and sing, we who have nothing to lose, and while behind their shutters boredom looms with slumped shoulders and bent brows, our noble folk gamble palaces and mistresses on a deal of the cards!

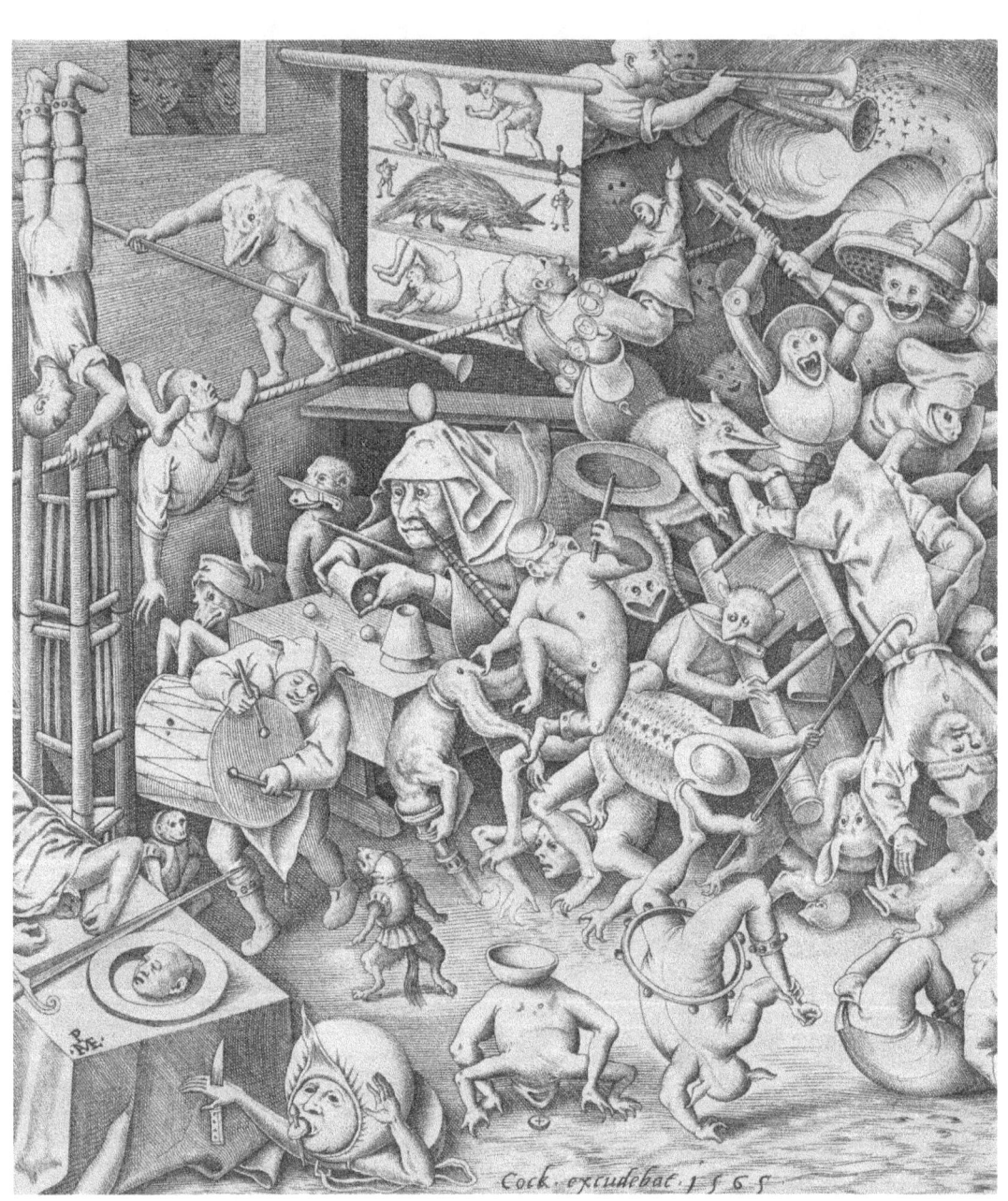

HERE ENDS THE FIFTH
BOOK OF THE FANTASIES
OF GASPARD
DE LA
NUIT.

HERE BEGINS THE SIXTH
BOOK OF THE FANTASIES
OF GASPARD
DE LA
NUIT.

SYLPHS

MY THATCHED COTTAGE

I.

In autumn, thrushes would come to rest there, attracted by the bright red berries of the mountain ash.
Baron R. Monthermé.

Upon looking up, the good old woman saw how the wind tormented the trees and erased traces of crows hopping on snow around the barn.
The German poet Voss. *Idyll XIII.*

MY THATCHED COTTAGE

My thatched cottage would have, in summer, the leaves of the woods for an awning, and in autumn, as a garden, outside my window, some moss that enshrines pearls of rain, and a few gillyflowers that blossom as if almond flowers.

But winter — what pleasure! when morning would have shivered its bouquets of frost on my frozen windowpanes, to see at some distance at the forest's edge a traveler who's always getting smaller and smaller, just him and his mount, in the snow and mist.

What pleasure! in evening, to leaf through the pages of the stories of valiant knights and monks by the blazing fireplace mantle scented with a bundle of juniper branches, portraits so vivid some seem to joust and others to pray anew.

And what pleasure! at night, at the uncertain and wan hour before daybreak, to hear my rooster crow in the henhouse and some rooster at a nearby farm answer him faintly, like a sentry perched at the outskirts of our sleeping village.

Ah! if only the king read our story in his Louvre — O my muse unsheltered from the storms of life! — the overlord reigning over so many fiefdoms, who doesn't know how many castles he has, would not haggle with us over one small cottage!

RIVER JOHN

II.

It's the trunk of an old willow tree and its bending branches.
H. DE LATOUCHE. *The King of the Alders.*

RIVER JOHN

"My ring, my ring!" — And then the scream of a frightened washerwoman. Inside a hollowed willow stump, a rat spinning its yarn.

Another of River John's tricks, the mischievous and wily swimmer who ripples, kvetches and laughs under repeated blows of the paddle!

As if it was not enough for him to harvest, from the dense patches of brush along the river bank, ripe medlars that he dunks in the current.

"John the thief! John who plays pranks and will be caught! Little John, who I dredged white with a shroud of flour frying away in the pan's sizzling oil!"

But then the crows, perched in the green spires of the poplars, cawed in the damp and rainy sky.

And the washerwomen, rigged out like shad fishermen, stepped across the ford littered with cobble, foam, weeds and gladioli.

To M. the Baron R.

OCTOBER

III.

Farewell, last beautiful days!
ALPH. DE LAMARTINE. *Autumn*.

OCTOBER

The little chimney sweeps are back, and their shouts already cut through the neighborhood's sonorous hum. Just as swallows follow spring, they usher in winter.

October, winter's harbinger, knocks at the door of our homes. An intermittent rain pelts dirty windowpanes, and the wind strews dead plane tree leaves on lonely stoops.

Now come family gatherings so enjoyable when everything outside is snow, ice and frost, and hyacinths bloom on mantles in the coziness of the parlor.

Now St. Martin's Day arrives and its firebrands, Christmas and its candles, New Year's Day and its games, All Kings Day and its broad beans, Carnival and its puppet shows.

And finally Easter, Easter with its exultant morning hymns, Easter when young girls receive the white host and red-colored eggs!

At that time a little ash on our foreheads will have rubbed away the boredom of six months of winter, and in due time the little chimney sweeps will greet again our tiny hamlet from the crest of the hill.

ON THE CRAGS OF CHÈVREMORTE

IV.

And I too have been ripped and torn by thorns in this desert, and I leave there each day another scrap of my skin.
Martyrs, Book X.

ON THE CRAGS OF CHÈVREMORTE*

It's not here that you inhale the scent of oak moss and poplar buds, it's not here that breezes and springs whisper love together.

No balm, in the morning, after rain, in the evening, in the hours when dew falls; and nothing charms the ear but the cry of a little bird scratching among blades of grass.

Desert that no longer carries the voice of John the Baptist, desert where neither hermits nor doves dwell!

And so my soul becomes a wasteland where, on the edge of the abyss, one hand grasps life and the other death, and I heave up a sorry sob.

The poet is like a gillyflower that attaches itself, delicate and fragrant, to granite, and demands less from earth than sun.

But alas! I've no more need of the sun, since such charming eyes have closed that kindled my genius!

22 June 1832.

* Half a league from Dijon.

ANOTHER SPRING

V.

All thoughts, all passions that move a mortal heart are slaves of love.
　　Coleridge.

ANOTHER SPRING

Another spring — another drop of dew that will slosh around for a moment in my bitter chalice and which escapes like a tear.

O my youth, your delights have been frozen by the kisses of time, but your sorrows have survived periods when they strangled your heart.

And you who unravelled the silk threads of my life, O women! If there were someone faithless in my love story, it wasn't me. If someone were betrayed, it wasn't you!

O spring! little bird of passage, our guest for a season who sings sadly in the poet's heart and on oak branches!

Another spring — another ray of May sun shining on a young poet's brow, out in the world, standing before an old oak, amid the woods!

Paris, 11 May 1836.

To M. A. de Latour.

SECOND MAN

VI.

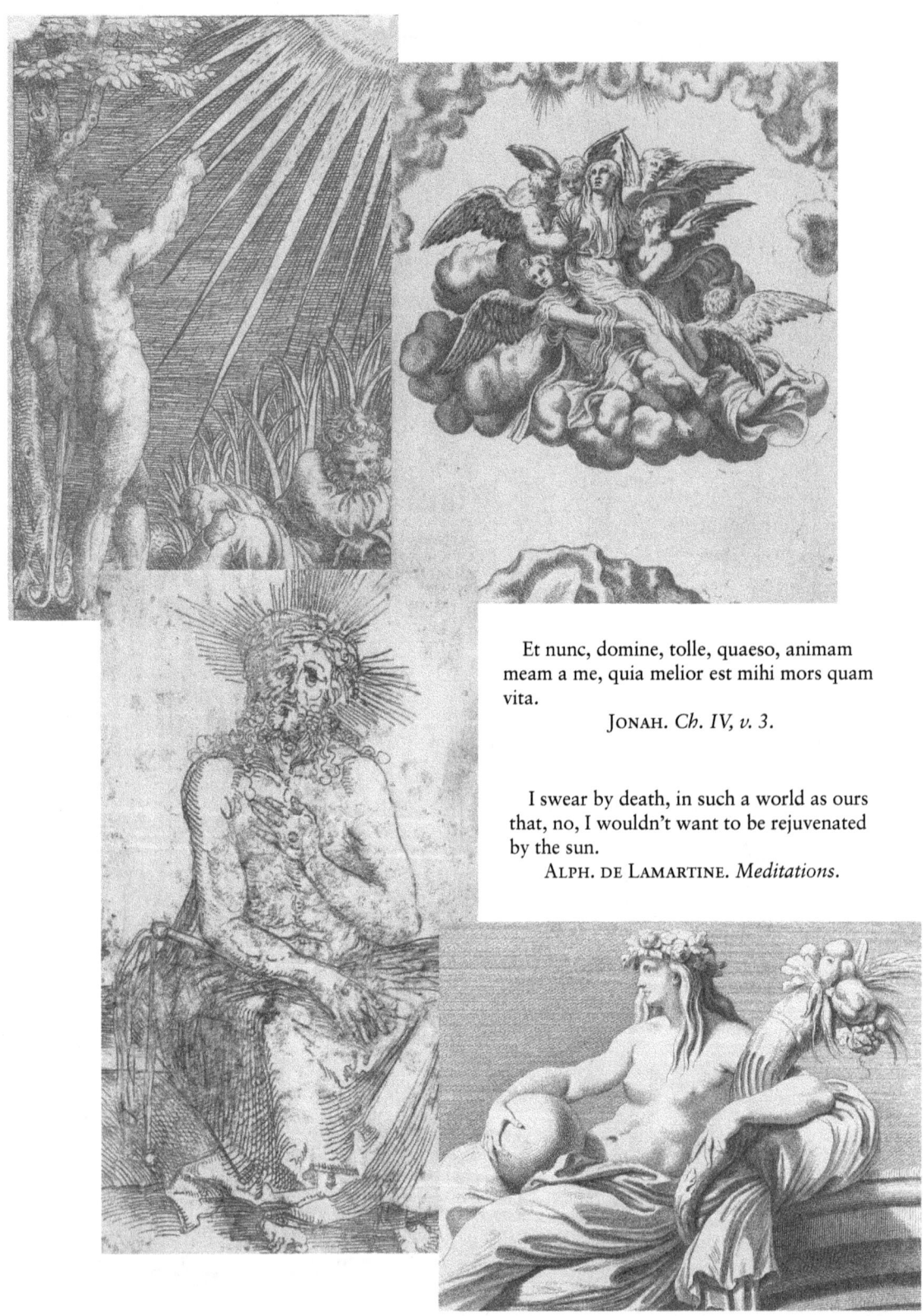

Et nunc, domine, tolle, quaeso, animam meam a me, quia melior est mihi mors quam vita.
                    JONAH. *Ch. IV, v. 3.*

I swear by death, in such a world as ours that, no, I wouldn't want to be rejuvenated by the sun.
                    ALPH. DE LAMARTINE. *Meditations.*

SECOND MAN

Hell! — Hell and heaven! — cries of despair! shouts of joy! — curses of the damned! songs of the chosen! — souls of the dead, mountain oaks uprooted by demons! dead souls as if valley flowers plucked by angels.

*

Sun, heaven, earth and man, everything began, everything ended. A voice bellowed in the nothingness. — "Sun!" called that voice from the gates of glorious Jerusalem. — "Sun!" reverberated the refrains from the inconsolable Jehoshaphat. — And the sun opened its golden eyelashes on the chaos of the universe.

But heaven hung like a tattered banner. — "Heaven!" called that voice from the gates of glorious Jerusalem. — "Heaven!" reverberated the refrains from the inconsolable Jehoshaphat. — And heaven unfurled folds of purple and azure into the winds.

But the earth drifted away, drifting like a battered ship that bears in its hold only ash and bone. "Earth!" called this voice from the gates of glorious Jerusalem. — "Earth!" reverberated the refrains from the inconsolable Jehoshaphat. — And the earth having cast anchor, nature disembarked, adorned with flowers, beneath a mountain portico with a hundred thousand columns.

But man was missing from this creation, and earth and nature were saddened, one from the absence of its king, the other from the absence of its spouse. — "Man!" called that voice from the gates of glorious Jerusalem. — "Man!" reverberated the refrains from the inconsolable Jehoshaphat. — And the hymn of deliverance and grace did not break the seal with which death had made fast the lips of the man sleeping for eternity on the tomb's bed.

"So be it!" exclaimed that voice, and the gates of glorious Jerusalem now open into two sepulchral corridors. — "So be it!" reverberated the refrains, and the inconsolable Jehoshaphat began to weep once more. — And the trumpet of the archangel resounded from abyss to abyss, while everything collapsed with a crash and became an immense ruin: heaven, earth and sun, lacking man, creation's cornerstone.

HERE ENDS THE SIXTH AND LAST
BOOK OF THE FANTASIES
OF GASPARD
DE LA
NUIT.

TO M. CHARLES NODIER.

I hope readers of this, my work, take to heart much of what I write here.
Memoirs of the Lord of Joinville.

TO M. CHARLES NODIER

Man is a minting machine who secretly strikes a coin in recondite sanctums. The coin bears the emperor's imprint, the medal's the pope's, the slug the madman's.

I mark my token in this game of life where we lose time after time and where the Devil, to put an end to it, makes off with players, dice and the green felt.

The emperor dictates his orders to his captains, the pope addresses bulls to Christendom, and a fool writes a book.

My book's here, such as it is, as I made it and as one must read it before critics bury it with their elucidations.

But these ill-conceived pages, humble labor little appreciated these days, might fail in their attempt to add some luster to the poetic reknown of days gone by.

And while the minstrel's wild rose may wither, the gillyflower always blooms every spring in the windows of Gothic castles and monasteries.

Paris, 20 September 1836.

End.

NOTES

TRANSLATOR'S AFTERWORD

THE CHIEF AIM OF THIS EDITION is to present to the reader *Gaspard de la Nuit* as Louis Bertrand envisioned it (albeit in English). Bertrand first gave to Eugène Renduel in 1836 the manuscript he wanted published. Renduel sat on the manuscript for several years, finally deciding not to publish it, citing that the time was not right to do so. Eventually Victor Pavie was convinced to take on the project in 1839, but it was not until early in 1841 that David d'Angers, Bertrand's friend, worked to retrieve the manuscript from Renduel and Pavie repaid Renduel's original advance. Unfortunately, Bertrand died in April 1841. *Gaspard* was published the following year, with some alterations by Pavie. In that first printed edition of *Gaspard*, Pavie swapped out "Captain Lazare" for the "Leyden Schoolboy" since the former offended Pavie's religious sensibilities. The edition also included a forward by Sainte-Beuve, as well as a number of prose poems Bertrand had written but did not include in his manuscript.

This edition is based on Bertrand's original manuscript, sent to Renduel, rescued by d'Angers and then used by Pavie (which was rediscovered in 1925). In this manuscript, "Captain Lazare" is retained, and there are some very minor textual differences to Pavie's published edition. Also, this edition is presented as how Bertrand wanted *Gaspard* presented textually. His manuscript consists of six books and ends with the final piece dedicated to Charles Nodier. Pavie also changed the dedication of this piece to Sainte-Beuve. It does not include other prose poems by Bertrand, even though they are some of his most famous works, among them "The Gibbet." The goal is to present the text of *Gaspard* as a whole, and not to serve as Bertrand's collected prose poems.

With his original manuscript, Bertrand provided the publisher, and the typesetter, with some very specific instructions on how he wanted his book to look. After all, these are fantasies in the manner of Rembrandt and Callot. How this book looks is just as important as what it says. Textually, Bertrand wanted extra space, akin to the spacing between stanzas of lineated poetry, between his paragraphs, and dialog. While most of the pieces are organized around usually five to seven paragraphs, he noted nine pieces in the second half of the manuscript that had dialog. It was his wish, if possible, to give space between these lines as well. That is done here.

Also in the manuscript Bertrand gave each title and epigraph its own separate page, and then repeated the title with the prose poem's text on the following manuscript page. That format is adhered to here, as part of Bertrand's visual presentation. Bertrand also embellished those titles and section markers with flourishes of the pen. I have included some of those here, regularizing them, again to provide a sense of how Bertrand presented his text.

The accuracy of Bertrand's epigraphs is sketchy at best. Some are misquoted, misremembered or mistranslated. A few may be fabricated. They are presented here with no correction or comment.

In addition, Bertrand made room for a Notes section in the manuscript, and on its table of contents. He supplied the concept, but no actual end notes. In his instructions he recognized that the book may not be long enough and some notes might be needed to stretch it out, but left that to fate. A blank Notes section is provided here — like a bodily appendix — and the reader may use this textual appendage as they want. However, Bertrand did provide some footnotes throughout his manuscript. They are retained here as he presented them, and are the only notes presented in this edition.

Bertrand also left some extensive instructions on illustrations. His instructions stated that "[t]he frame should be capacious [in the use of white space] and as embellished as possible." He specifically called for one illustration of a Dijon clock tower that is included at the beginning of this edition. He also called for an artist (or artists) to draw specific tableaux for pieces. For example, for "Gothic Chamber" he asked that a drawing represent "the earth as a flower whose calyx . . . are topped with the moon and stars." Ideally, one would want to be able to commission an artist, or artists, to follow his requests. Unfortunately, at this time that was beyond our means. Perhaps one day. Instead, artworks (chiefly drawings, engravings and etchings, with a few paintings) were chosen that related to the sensibilities of the book: the Gothic (primarily from the XIVth to XVIIth centuries) and from artists noted in the title (Callot and Rembrandt figure highly), but also those mentioned throughout the book. Almost everything are period pieces, except for a few dozen but most notably Bob Heman's collages. Bertrand also did some drawings, which have affinities to *Gaspard*. Those are included in this edition. Bertrand ended his instructions on the artwork by challenging the layout designer: "The more chaotic the arrangement of illustrations, the better the effect." The goal in this edition was to present as many images as possible (Bertrand's jumble) but with suitable amounts of white space. Also, the images should help illuminate aspects of the pieces they are close to. I have only come across one edition, a 1903 edition published by the Société d'Editions d'Art that attempts to more fully integrate images with the text. That edition was illustrated by Jules Fontanez. Most of his pieces are included here; predominantly but not all near the pieces they originally appeared with. A list of illustrations, with artist and title, follows at the end of this edition.

So, while the chief aim of this edition — in terms of publishing — is to present the manuscript of *Gaspard* as closely possible to what Bertrand envisioned, another goal of the translation was to follow his character and, above all, Bertrand's poetry — its sound, rhythm and sense. *Gaspard* is full of history, cultural allusions and puns that draw on Bertrand's knowledge of the Gothic period as well as his own. On the one hand, to translate Bertrand well, one would need to include layers upon layers of explanatory notes. On that level, there is an incredible amount of richness. However, here, as translator, I sought to have Bertrand, the poet, speak without filter, and without explanation or explication. Yes, much will be lost, but I am hoping that I have brought out Bertrand's *poetry* and his liveliness — what endeared him to the literati of his time. For those who want to dive into the richness of the contexts that Bertrand mines, there are two other excellent annotated and explicated editions: John T. Wright's translation published in 1994 by the University Press of America; and Donald Sydney-Fryer's translation published in 2004 by Black Coat Press. Both editions provide very good biographical information on Bertrand as well.

In terms of the practicalities of being as faithful to Bertrand's text as possible, I need to note that some liberties have been taken. First, and most importantly, poetic effect and sense were given a priority. There are occasions where to best convey a passage in English, some detachment from the sense of the original French was made. Next, Bertrand's punctuation was less than consistent and would be highly confusing to the modern English reader. Punctuation for dialog was normalized, and narrative punctuation reduced to where it was necessary, especially for rhythm. As much of Bertrand's frequent and quixotic use of dashes was retained as possible. Bertrand also used an abundance of periods for section and poem titles. I have retained a semblance of that here, but not to the extent Bertrand used. Last, most place and personal names were kept in French unless the English reader would be more comfortable with a better-known English version (for example, St. Peter's).

The goal here was to make Louis Bertrand come alive as an inventive and revolutionary prose poet. I hope I have achieved that goal. The reader, as always, is the final arbiter in that regard.

Gian Lombardo.

LIST OF ILLUSTRATIONS

The artwork herein was sourced from the public domain or via Creative Common license, or by permission. To save space, the following acronyms identify where an image comes from: Albertina Museum [AM], Archives Nationale (France) [AN], Art Gallery NSW [AG], Art Institute Chicago [AIC], Bibliotèques Municipales d'Angers [BMA], British Museum [BM], Gallica [G], Kunsthistorisches Museum [KM], Library of Congress [LC], Maison de Victor Hugo [MVH], Metropolitan Museum of Art (New York City) [MMA], Musée Carnavalet [MC], Musée Gustave Moreau [MGM], Museum of Fine Arts (Houston) [MFAH], National Gallery of Art [NGA], New York Public Library [NYPL], Petit Palais [PP], Rijksmuseum [R], Royal Museum of Fine Arts Antwerp [RMFAA], the 1903 edition of *Gaspard de la Nuit* (Société d'Editions d'Art) [SEA], Städel Museum [SM], Teylers Museum [TM], Wellcome Collection [WC], Wikimedia Commons [WMC] and Yale Center for British Art [YCBA].

I: *Rembrandt and Callot*, illustration by Jules Fontanez (1903) SEA.

II: *Jacquemart of Dijon*, from *Pittoresque* magazine (1834).

IV: *Garden of the Arquebus, Dijon*, photo by Jean François Maillard digitally altered (2022).

V: Portion of *Arquebus Training Exercise: Firing*, etching by Jacques Callot (1635) MMA.

VIII: *Biron Relieves Dijon for Henry VI, 1595*, etching from workshop of Frans Hogenberg (ca. 1595) R.

IX: Portion of *Is this an enchantment. . .* etching by Claude Gillot (early 1700s) MMA.

X: *View of Dijon*, etching by Hendrik Roosing (ca. 1786) R.

XXVI: *Snake ornament*, anonymous engraving (n.d.).

XXVII (top): *Bust of Janus*, etching by Gerard van Groeningen, possibly after Hans Vredeman de Vries (1573) MMA.

XXVII (bottom): *Punchinello With Dumpling or Fritter*, drawing and wash by circle of Giovanni Battista Tiepolo (1696–1770) MMA.

XXVIII: *The Family*, etching by Adriaen van Ostade (1610–1685) MMA.

XXX: Playing card, with *Wild Woman and Unicorn*, engraving by Master ES (15th century) MMA.

xxxi: *Fable of the Old Stork*, etching by Aegidius Sadeler (1608) R.

xxxii (top): *Victor Hugo*, lithograph by Antoine Maurin (before 1837) MVH.

xxxii (bottom): A page from "News of the Day" in *Le Charivari*, lithograph by Honoré Daumier (November 16, 1870) MMA.

xxxiii: Portion of *Friezes With Birds, Flowers and Meandering Wreaths and Scrolls*, etching by Theodor Bang (ca. 1600–1617) MMA.

xxxiv: *Departure for the Sabbath*, illustration by Jules Fontanez (1903) SEA.

1: *The Watchful Eye*, etching by Jacques Callot (1621–1635) MMA.

2: *The Haunting*, collage by Bob Heman (2022).

3: *The Death of Sin Brings a New Person to Life*, etching by Dirck Volckertsz Coornhert (1550) R.

4: *Haarlem*, illustration by Jules Fontanez (1903) SEA.

5: *View of the Zander Tower in Haarlem, 1640*, etching by Abraham Rademaker (1727–1733) R.

6 (top): *Jan Smit Hung on One Leg in Haarlem, 1572*, etching by Jan Luyken (1685) R.

6 (bottom): *Main Gate in Haarlem*, etching by Abraham Rademaker (1727–1733) R.

7: Detail from *The Virgin and Child Enthroned*, painting by the Master of the Embroidered Foliage (ca. 1500), photo by Gian Lombardo.

8: *The Mason*, illustration by Jules Fontanez (1903) SEA.

9: *Cathedral Flying Buttresses*, photo by Rodney Bamford digitally altered (2022).

10 (top left): *A Mounted Drummer From the Front*, drawing by Marcellus Laroon the Elder (1670–1702) MMA.

10 (top right): *Gargoyle From La Sainte-Chapelle*, Paris (n.d.) WMC.

10 (bottom): Portion of *Looting and Burning of a Village*, etching by Jacques Callot (1636) MMA.

12: *Schoolboy of Leyden*, illustration by Jules Fontanez (1903) SEA.

13: *A Lansquenet*, etching by Sebald Beham (1520) MMA.

14 (top): *The Moneylender*, painting by Gerard Dou (1664) WMC.

14 (bottom): *A Rat-Catcher in Haarlem*, anonymous etching (17th century) WC.

15: Portion of *Hofhuis: Interior, Velours of Utrecht*, photo by G. de Hoog (1909) Rijksdienst voor het Cultureel Erfgoed.

16: *Pointed Beard*, illustration by Jules Fontanez (1903) SEA.

17: *The Talmud Students*, engraving by Ephraim Moses Lilien (1915) WMC.

18 (top): *Man With Pointed Beard*, drawing by Louis Bertrand (1830s) BMA.

18 (bottom): *Jews in a Synagogue*, etching after Rembrandt (1648) MMA.

20. *Tulip Peddler*, illustration by Jules Fontanez (1903) SEA.

21: *Two Tulips With Two Damselflies and Ladybug*, pencil and watercolor by Jacob Marrel (1639) R.

22 (top): *Passion Flower*, anonymous drawing (n.d.) WC.

22 (middle): *Luther Nailing His Thesis to the Door*, anonymous engraving (1882) WMC.

22 (bottom): *Portrait of the Third Duke of Alba*, painting by Antonis Mor (1549) WMC.

24: *Five Fingers of the Hand*, illustration by Jules Fontanez (1903) SEA.

25: *A Family Carousing*, drawing by David Teniers the Younger (17th century) MMA.

26 (top): *Gillyflowers*, watercolor by J. Eudes (before 1929) WMC.

26 (bottom): *Male Peasant Smoking a Pipe*, etching after David Tenier the Younger (1625–1690) MMA.

27: Portion of *Studies of Heads*, engraving with etching by Battista Franco (16th century) MMA.

28: *Viol da Gamba*, illustration by Jules Fontanez (1903) SEA.

29: *Viola da Gamba Player*, engraving by Hans Sebald Beham (1520) NYPL.

30: *Pierrot*, lithograph by Clément Pruche (19th century) MC.

31: Detail from *Four Putti*, engraving by the Master of the Die, after Raphael (ca. 1530–1540) MMA.

32: *The Alchemist*, illustration by Jules Fontanez (1903) SEA.

33: *The Alchemist*, engraving by Pieter Bruegel the Elder (after 1558) MMA.

34: *An Alchemist*, painting by Adriaen van Ostade (1661) WMC.

35: *Raymond Lulle*, engraving by Balthasar Moncornet (17th century) NGA.

36 (all three): *Drawings of Maribas* by Louis Bertrand (1830s) BMA.

37: *Witches' Sabbath*, drawing by Salvator Rosa (1615–1673) MMA.

38: *Departure for the Sabbath*, etching after David Teniers the Younger, by Baron Dominique Vivant Denon (late 1700s) MMA.

39: *A Spider*, watercolor by Jan Vincentsz van der Vinne (late 1600s/early 1700s) MMA.

40: *Witches' Sabbath*, drawing by Salvator Rosa (1640–1649) MMA.

41: *Death and the Lansquenet*, woodcut by Albrecht Dürer (1510) MMA.

42: *The Cult of the Demon*, etching by Jacques Callot (ca. 1625) MMA.

43 (top): *Donjon of John the Fearless, Paris*, illustration by Henri Chapelle (1905) MC.

43 (bottom): *Boulevard du Temple, Paris*, photo by Louis Daguerre (1838).

44: *Two Jews*, illustration by Juless Fontanez (1903) SEA.

45: *A Drunken Street Brawl*, anonymous etching (?16th century) WC.

46: *Two Jews in Discussion*, drawing by Rembrandt (between 1626 and 1669) TM.

47: Detail from *A True and Thorough Instruction in Geometry*, etching by Augustin Hirschvogel (1543) MMA.

48: *Night Tramps*, illustration by Jules Fontanez (1903) SEA.

49: *Men by a Campfire*, engraving by Dirck Bosboom (ca. 1674–1685) R.

50 (top): *Eight Beggars*, etching after Jacques Callot by Wenceslaus Hollar (1630) MMA.

50 (middle): *Pietro dal Monte*, engraving by Jacques Callot (1611–1619) MMA.

50 (bottom): *Six Beggars at a Fountain*, etching by Jan van Ossenbeeck (1647–1674) R.

52: *Lantern*, illustration by Jules Fontanez (1903) SEA.

53 (left): Portion of *Night, Woman With Lantern*, drawing by Gesina ter Borch (ca. 1655) R.

53 (right): *A Girl Singing Ballads by a Paper Lantern*, mezzotint by Thomas Watson (1767–1781) MMA.

54 (top): *The Hellmouth*, etching and engraving by Mathäus Küsel (1668) MMA.

54 (bottom): *The Fish and the Fireworks*, etching by Lamotte-Houdar (1719) MMA.

55: Manuscript ornament, drawing by Louis Bertrand (1830s).

56: *Nesle Tower*, illustration by Jules Fontanez (1903) SEA.

57: *Man Adjusting His Footwear, at Left Three Men Playing Cards*, etching by Thomas Wijck (1630–1677) MMA.

58 (top): *Old Paris 15th/16th Century, View Near Nesle Tower*, etching by François Alexandre Pernot (1835–1836) MVH.

58 (bottom): Portion of *Hope*, engraving by Philips Galle, after Pieter Bruegel the Elder (1559–1560) MMA.

59: Detail of *Queen of Spades*, playing card made by W. Duke, Sons & Co. (1888) MMA.

60: *A Refined Person*, illustration by Jules Fontanez (1903) SEA.

61: *The Gentleman With a Fur Shirt Front*, etching by Jacques Callot (ca. 1623) MMA.

62 (top): *Three Violets*, anonymous engraving (1787–1789) R.

62 (bottom): Portion of *The Ill-Matched Couple*, engraving by Albrecht Dürer (n.d.) MMA.

64: *Evening Prayers*, illustration by Jules Fontanez (1903) SEA.

65: *Interior of a Gothic Church at Night*, painting by Pieter Neeffs the Elder and Frans Francken (ca. 1635–1640) WMC.

66 (top): *Couple in Window*, drawing by Louis Bertrand (1830s) BMA.

66 (bottom): *Studies of Kneeling Figures*, drawing and wash by Salvator Rosa (1615–1673) MMA.

67: Portion of *Ornament With Two Sirens*, engraving by Lucas van Leyden (1528) MMA.

68: *The Musicians*, engraving by Lucas van Leyden (1524) MMA.

69: *Night Watchers*, woodcut by Albrecht Dürer (1494) WMC.

70 (left): *Guitar Player*, illustration by Louis Bertrand (1830s) BMA.

70 (right): *Gentleman*, illustration by Louis Bertrand (1830s) BMA.

72: *Sir John*, illustration by Jules Fontanez (1903) SEA.

73: Portion of *Five Figures in Fantastic Costumes With Two Dogs*, drawing by Salvator Rosa (1615–1673) MMA.

74 (top): Portion of *Noble Woman With Large Collar*, etching by Jacques Callot (ca. 1620–1623) WMC.

74 (bottom): *Studies of Hounds*, drawings by David Teniers the Younger (17th century) MMA.

75: *Coat of Arms With a Mask, Held by Two Genii*, engraving by Lucas van Leyden (1527) MMA.

76: *Midnight Mass*, illustration by Jules Fontanez (1903) SEA.

77: *June (The Pentecostblom)*, engraving by Cornelis Dusart (1679–1704) R.

78: *Interior of a Gothic Church by Night*, painting by Pieter Neeffs (1636) WMC.

79: Portion of *The Lamentation*, drawing by the circle of Jan de Beer (ca. 1500–1520) MMA.

80: *Bibliophile*, illustration by Jules Fontanez (1903) SEA.

81: *The Very Rich Hours of the Duke of Berry, June*, illuminated manuscript possibly by the Limbourg Brothers (ca. 1412) WMC.

82 (top): *Scholar Sharpening a Quill Pen*, painting by Gerrit Dou (ca. 1632–1635) WMC.

82 (bottom): *Faust*, etching by Rembrandt (ca. 1652) MMA.

83: *View of the Pont Neuf*, etching by Israël Silvestre (1631–1661) R.

84 (top): *Misanthrope Robbed by the World*, engraving by Jan Wierex, after Pieter Bruegel the Elder (ca. 1568) MMA.

84 (bottom): *Big Fish Eat Little Fish*, engraving by Pieter van der Heyden, after Pieter Bruegel the Elder (1557) MMA.

85: *Map of Paris, Ile de la Cité and Notre-Dame*, anonymous engraving (n.d.) AN.

86: Portion of *Fireworks at Hemissem*, etching and drypoint by Wenceslaus Hollar (ca. 1650) MMA.

87: *The Eclipse*, collage by Bob Heman (2022).

88: *Self Portrait in a Cap With Eyes Wide Open*, etching print by Rembrandt (1630) WMC.

89: *The Tomb*, etching by Jacques Callot (1621–1635) MMA.

90: *The Nightmare*, engraving by Thomas Holloway, after the painting by Henry Fuseli (1791) WC.

91: Manuscript ornament, drawing by Louis Bertrand (1830s).

92: *Man Leering*, etching by Adriaen van Ostade (1610–1685) MMA.

93: *Scarbo*, illustration by Louis Bertrand (1830s) BMA.

94 (top): *Masked Dwarf With Contorted Legs*, etching and engraving by Jacques Callot (1620) SM.

94 (bottom): *The Death of Infants*, etching by Bartolomeo Pinelli (1825) WC.

95: Manuscript ornament, drawing by Louis Bertrand (1830s).

96: Portion of *Two Fools Dancing*, engraving by Hendrick Hondius (1642) MMA.

97: *Clown*, illustration by Louis Bertrand (1830s) BMA.

98 (top): *Weathervane*, photo by Bicanski digitally altered and cropped (2022).

98 (middle): *The Raven and the Snail*, etching by Jacques Callot (1621–1635) MMA.

98 (bottom): *The Miser*, etching by Wencelaus Hollar, after Hans Holbein the Younger (1651) MMA.

99: Detail from *Battle Between Cavalry and Infantry in a Wood*, etching by Hieronymus Hopfer (16th century) MMA.

100: *The Changeling*, drawing by Henry Fuseli (ca. 1780) AIC.

101: *Wrapped in Cocoon*, drawing by Louis Bertrand (1830s) BMA.

102 (top): *The Great South Sea Caterpillar Transformed Into a Bath Butterfly*, etching by James Gillray (1795) LC.

102 (middle): *Dwarves and a Donkey*, etching by Stefano della Bella (1620–1664) R.

102 (bottom): *Study of a Galloping Horse*, anonymous drawing (1800–1899) YCBA.

103: Portion of *The Visit to the Spinner*, engraving by Israhel van Meckenem (ca. 1495–1503) NGA.

104: *Moonlight*, illustration by Jules Fontanez (1903) SEA.

105: *Moon and Bell*, drawing by Louis Bertrand (1830s) BMA.

106 (top): *Moon and Clown*, drawing by Louis Bertrand (1830s) BMA.

106 (bottom): *Two Men Seen Three-Quarter Length*, drawing/wash by Salvator Rosa (1615–1673) MMA.

107: Portion of *Two Soldiers With Lance and Halberd Conversing*, woodcut by Hans Schäufelein (ca. 1515) MMA.

108: *Patrol Beneath the Bell*, illustration by Jules Fontanez (1903) SEA.

109: Portion of *Circle of Magicians in the Chamber of Presence*, anonymous etching (1639) MMA.

110 (top): *The Romance of the Rose*, illuminated manuscript (1390) WMC.

110 (middle): *Sabbath Roundelay*, lithograph by Louis Boulanger (1828) MVH.

110 (bottom): *Landscape With a Square Tower*, etching and drypoint by Rembrandt (1650) MMA.

112: *A Dream*, illustration by Jules Fontanez (1903) SEA.

113: *The Executioner*, engraving by Jacques Callot (1611–1619) MMA.

114 (top): Portion of *The Wheel*, etching by Jacques Callot (1633) AG.

114 (bottom): Portion of *The Hanging*, etching by Jacques Callot (1633) MMA.

116: *My Great-Grandfather*, illustration by Jules Fontanez (1903) SEA.

117: *Head of an Old Man*, drawing by Albrecht Dürer (1521) WMC.

118 (top): *Old Man*, drawing by Louis Bertrand (1830s) BMA.

118 (bottom): *The Nightmare*, lithograph by Cham (1855) MC.

119: Portion of *Old Couple and Death With Bagpipes*, etching with engraving by Werner van den Valckert (1612) MMA.

120: *Ondine*, illustration by Jules Fontanez (1903) SEA.

121: *Sleeping Woman With a Cupid*, etching and drypoint by Henry Fuseli (1780–1790) MMA.

122 (top): *The Reed and the Wind*, etching by Jacques Callot (1621–1635) MMA.

122 (bottom): *Nymph Playing a Horn*, anonymous drawing and wash (16th century) MMA.

124: *Salamander*, illustration by Jules Fontanez (1903) SEA.

125: *Candle-Blowing Man*, etching by Cornelis Ploos van Amstel (1782–1787) R.

126 (top): *Talking Cricket*, illustration by Enrico Mazzanti (1883) WMC.

126 (middle): *Farmers in an Inn*, etching by Cornelis de Wael (1630–1648) R.

126 (bottom): *Study of an Interior With a Stove*, etching by Gerard Jan Bos (ca. 1878–1885) R.

127: Portion of *Grisaille Glass With Grotesques*, anonymous painted glass (ca. 1320–1324) MMA.

128: *The Witch*, engraving by Albrecht Dürer (ca. 1500) MMA.

129 (left): *Hanged Man With Moon*, drawing by Louis Bertrand (1830s) BMA.

129 (right): *Elsje Christiaens Hanging on a Gibbet*, drawing and wash by Rembrandt (1664) MMA.

130 (top): *November*, anonymous drawing (17th century) R.

130 (bottom): *A Wild Cat Climbing Down a Tree in a Forest*, etching by J. E. Ridinger (18th century) WC.

131: Portion of *1 of Nooses Playing Card*, anonymous (ca. 1475–1480) MMA.

132: *Dwarf*, illustration by Jules Fontanez (1903) SEA.

133: *The Sea Monster*, engraving by Albrecht Dürer (ca. 1498) MMA.

134 (top): *Landscape*, print by Hans Bol (16th century) MMA.

134 (bottom): *Two Gossips*, etching by Adriaen van Ostade (1610–1685) MMA.

135: *Some Construction*, collage by Bob Heman (2022).

136: *Master Ogier*, illustration by Jules Fontanez (1903) SEA.

137 (top): *Parable of the Workers in the Vineyard*, engraving by Jan Collaert (1597) R.

137 (middle): *Ball of the Burning Men*, anonymous illustration (n.d.) WMC.

137 (bottom): *Charles VI, King of France*, engraving by Nicolas de Larmessin (1690) G.

138 (top): *Tree and Column*, illustration by Louis Bertrand (1830s) BMA.

138 (bottom): Portion of *Composite Design of Grapes and Grape Leaves*, block print by William Blake (19th century) Smithsonian Design Museum.

140: *Louvre Private Entrance*, illustration by Jules Fontanez (1903) SEA.

141: Portion of *View of the Louvre*, etching by Jacques Callot (ca. 1630) MMA.

142 (top): *Small Male Figure in Profile View*, etching by Jacques Callot (ca. 1621–1625) MMA.

142 (middle): *Swiss Guard*, anonymous etching (ca. 1750) R.

142 (bottom): *Nesle Tower*, illustration by Henri Chapelle (late 1800s) MC.

144: *The Old Louvre*, etching by Charles Méryon (1865–1866) MMA.

145: *The Standard Bearer*, engraving by Lucas van Leyden (ca. 1510) MMA.

146: *The Flemish*, illustration by Jules Fontanez (1903) SEA.

148: *The Hunt*, illustration by Jules Fontanez (1903) SEA.

149: *Two Squires*, etching by Jacques Callot (1621–1635) MMA.

150 (top): *Stag Lying to Left*, etching by Wenceslaus Hollar, after Albrecht Dürer (1649) MMA.

150 (bottom): Portion of *The Stag Hunt*, etching by Jacques Callot (1619) MFAH.

152: *Black Riders*, illustration by Jules Fontanez (1903) SEA.

153: *Reiter and Captives*, drawing by Gustave Moreau (late 1800s) MGM.

154 (top): *A Man Helping a Rider to Mount a Horse*, drawing by Rembrandt (ca. 1641–1642) WMC.

154 (middle): *Two Franciscan Monks*, painting by Bartolomé Estaban Murillo (ca. 1645–1647) WMC.

154 (bottom): *Knight, Death and Devil*, engraving by Albrecht Dürer (1513) NGA.

155: Detail from *Virgin and Child*, painting by Sandro Botticelli (ca. 1490), photo by Gian Lombardo.

156: *Dreaming of the River*, collage by Bob Heman (2022).

157: *The Camp*, etching by Jacques Callot (1636) MMA.

158: *Illustrious Detachments #1*, illustration by Jules Fontanez (1903) SEA.

159: Detail from *Coat of Arms With Cock*, engraving by Albrecht Dürer (ca. 1502) MMA.

160: *Illustrious Detachments #2*, illustration by Jules Fontanez (1903) SEA.

162: *Illustrious Detachments #3*, illustration by Jules Fontanez (1903) SEA.

163: *Quivers and Hunting Horns*, etching by Wenceslaus Hollar (1647) MMA.

164: *Lepers*, illustration by Jules Fontanez (1903) SEA.

165: *The Almshouse*, etching by Jacques Callot (1617) MMA.

166: *The Leper*, etching by Rembrandt (ca. 1629) R.

168: *The Falconer*, etching by Jacques Callot (1617) MMA.

169: *St. Jerome in His Study*, engraving by Lucas van Leyden (1521) MMA.

170 (top): *Arnold Tholinx, Inspector*, etching by Rembrandt (ca. 1650) WMC.

170 (bottom): *Self-Portrait*, Henry Fuseli (ca. 1777–1779) National Portrait Gallery.

171: *Opera Poster*, lithograph by Bertrand (18th century) MC.

172: *Saint John Devouring the Book*, woodcut by Albrecht Dürer (1498) MMA.

173: *The Tower of Babel*, painting by Pieter Brueghel the Elder (1553) WMC.

174 (top): *Three Warriors Conversing*, etching and drypoint by Salvator Rosa (ca. 1656–1657) MMA.

174 (bottom): Portion of *The Spanish Gypsy "Preciosa,"* etching by Rembrandt (ca. 1642) MMA.

175: *Artist Moved to Despair*, drawing by Henry Fuseli (1778–1780) WMC.

176: *The Cell*, illustration by Jules Fontanez (1903) SEA.

177: *The Hermit Praying*, painting by Gerrit Dou (1630) NGA.

178 (top): *Hypocaust in Pompeii*, etching by Francesco Piranesi (1805) R.

178 (bottom): *The Stopping Place of the Gypsies: The Fortune Tellers*, etching by Jacques Callot (1621–1631) MMA.

180: *Mule Drivers*, illustration by Jules Fontanez (1903) SEA.

181: *The Peasant Striking His Donkey*, etching by Jacques Callot (1621–1635) MMA.

182 (top): *A Coach*, drawing by Rembrandt (ca. 1660–1663) BM.

182 (bottom): *Studies of Animals*, painting and drawing by Jan Breughel the Elder (1616) KM.

184: Portion of *The Marching Gypsies: The Rear Guard*, etching by Jacques Callot (ca. 1592–1635) MMA.

185 (top): Portion of *The Attack on the Stagecoach*, etching by Jacques Callot (1633) MMA.

185 (bottom): *Attack en Route*, etching by Jacques Callot (1636) MMA.

186: *Marquis D'Aroca*, illustration by Jules Fontanez (1903) SEA.

188: *Henriquez*, illustration by Jules Fontanez (1903) SEA.

189: *The Cave of Thieves*, etching by Jacques Callot (1617) MMA.

190 (top): *Salvator Rosa Among the Brigands*, etching and aquatint by Adolphe Pierre Riffaut (after 1844) MMA.

190 (bottom): Portion of *The Discovery of the Criminals*, etching by Jacques Callot (1633) MMA.

191: Detail from *The Battle About Money*, engraving by Pieter van der Heyden (after 1570) MMA.

192 (top): *Tric Trac Players*, etching by Adriaen van Ostade (1610–1685) MMA.

192 (bottom): *The Barn*, etching by Adriaen van Ostade (1647) MMA.

193: *The Dance at the Inn*, etching by Adriaen van Ostade (1652) MMA.

194 (top): *The Inn*, etching by Jacques Callot (1617) MMA.

194 (bottom): *Soldiers and Girls Carousing*, drawing by Rembrandt (ca. 1635) WMC.

195: Portion of *Peacock and Raven*, engraving by Meister der Berliner Passion (1450–1475) AM.

196 (top): *View of the Exterior of St. Peter's Basilica*, etching by Giovanni Battista Piranesi (ca. 1748) MMA.

196 (bottom): *Death and the Devil Surprising Two Women*, etching by Daniel Hopfer (ca. 1515) MMA.

197: *St. Saturninus, Priest and His Companions*, etching by Jacques Callot (1636) MMA.

198 (top): *Maria Trip*, illustration by Rembrandt (1639) WMC.

198 (bottom): Portion of *Portrait of Johann Alten, of the Swiss Guard*, etching by Francesco Villamena (1623) MMA.

199: Detail from *Joachim and the Angel*, drawing by Anton Möller the Elder, after Albrecht Dürer (1582) MMA.

200: *Masked Canto*, illustration by Jules Fontanez (1903) SEA.

201: *Franca Trippa and Fritellino*, etching by Jacques Callot (after 1622) MMA.

202 (top): *View of St. Mark's Place in Venice*, woodcut by Jost Amman, after Albrecht Dürer (16th century) PP.

202 (middle): Portion of *The Lady With a Mask*, etching by Jacques Callot (ca. 1623) MMA.

202 (bottom): Portion of *Masquerade Dance With Torches*, woodcut by Albrecht Dürer (n.d.) MMA.

203: Portion of *The Church of Santa Maria della Salute Seen Across the Water With Gondolas*, etching by Michele Marieschi (1741) MMA.

204: Portion of *The Fall of the Magician*, engraving by Pieter van der Heyden (1565) MMA.

205: *French Bed*, etching and drypoint by Rembrandt (1646) R.

206: *Carefree in Poverty*, anonymous stained glass (1510–1520) MMA.

207 (top): *Sun*, etching by Master I. B. (1528) MMA.

207 (bottom): *St. Jerome in the Wilderness*, woodcut by Nicolò Boldrini, after Titian (mid-16th century) MMA.

208: *My Thatched Cottage*, illustration by Jules Fontanez (1903) SEA.

209 (right): *Two Figures on a Winding Path in a Forest*, etching by Jan Ruyscher (1648–1674) R.

209 (left): *Forest*, illustration by Louis Bertrand (1830s) BMA.

210: Portion of *Landscape With Cottage*, drawing in the manner of Jacques Callot (early 17th century) MMA.

212: *River John*, illustration by Jules Fontanez (1903) SEA.

213: *Preparations*, collage by Bob Heman (2022).

214 (top): *Landscape With a Herdsman*, etching and drypoint by Salvator Rosa (ca. 1640–1645) MMA.

214 (bottom): *Two Anglers on a Bridge*, etching by Adriaen van Ostade (1647) MMA.

215: *The Willows at the Waterfront*, etching by Jacques Callot (1621–1635) MMA.

216: *Dance Savoyard*, tapestry by Lecler, Père et Fils (ca. 1790) MMA.

217: *The Corn Harvest*, painting by Pieter Breugel the Elder (1565) WMC.

218 (top): *Autumn and Winter*, anonymous etching (ca. 1580–1620) MMA.

218 (middle): *Chimney Sweep*, engraving by Jan Matham (1628–1648) R.

218 (bottom): *Winter Landscape With Skaters and Bird Trap*, painting by Pieter Breughel the Elder (1565) WMC.

219: Portion of *The Miraculous Mass of St. Martin of Tours With the Apparition of a Ball of Fire Above His Head*, drawing by Giovanni Lanfranco (1582–1647) MMA.

220 (top): *Lion Standing Under a Mountain Crag*, anonymous etching and engraving (1668) WC.

220 (bottom): *Saint John Preaching in the Desert*, etching by Jacques Callot (1634–1635) MMA.

221: *Mill at Chèvremorte*, anonymous painting (n.d.).

222 (top): *St. John the Baptist in the Desert*, engraving by Lucas van Leyden (1513) MMA.

222 (bottom): *A Mountainous Landscape With Travelers on a Road*, drawing and wash by Jan van Aken (ca. 1650–1655) MMA.

223: Portion of *The Two Hearts*, etching by Jacques Callot (1621–1635) MMA.

224: Portion of *Spring*, drawing by Pieter Breugel the Elder (1565) WMC.

225: *Spring*, etching by Wenceslaus Hollar (1641) R.

226 (top): *Forest Glen*, illustration by Louis Bertrand (1830s) BMA.

226 (middle): *Spring and Summer*, anonymous etching (ca. 1580–1620) MMA.

226 (bottom): *Square Panel With Vegetal Scrollwork, Flowers and Fruits*, engraving by Bernhard Zan (1581) MMA.

227: *Anne of Austria*, etching by Stefano della Bella (1644) MMA.

228: *Saint Barbara*, drawing and painting by Jan van Eyck (1437) RMFAA.

229: *Hell*, engraving by Abraham van Diepenbeeck (1655) MMA.

230 (top left): *An Old Man on the Ground and a Young Man Pointing at the Sun, Leaning on an Anchor*, engraving by Marcantonio Raimondi (ca. 1510–1527) MMA.

230 (top right): *Mary Magdalene Carried to Heaven*, etching by Léon Davent (mid-16th century) MMA.

230 (bottom left): *The Man of Sorrows*, etching by Albrecht Dürer (1515) MMA.

230 (bottom right): *Earth*, engraving by Johann Justin Preissler (1735) MMA.

232 (left): *Josaphat*, woodcut by Michel Wolgemut (1493) R.

232 (right): *Joachim Embracing Saint Anne Under the Golden Gate in Jerusalem*, engraving by Marcantonio Raimondi, after Albrecht Dürer (ca. 1500–1534) MMA.

233: *Roundel With Three Apes Building a Trestle Table*, anonymous painted glass (1480–1500) MMA.

234 (top): *A Fool and a Woman*, etching and engraving by Lucas van Leyden (1520) MMA.

234 (bottom): *Tableau of Skeletons and Body Parts*, engraving by Frederik Ruysch (1703) WC.

235: *The Gamesters*, etching after Hans Holbein the Younger by Wenceslaus Hollar (1651) MMA.

236 (top): *Charles Nodier*, lithograph by François Seraphin Delpech (1835) MVH.

236 (bottom): *Gateway to the Abbey of St. Martin of Auchi*, lithograph by Louis Marie Jean Baptiste Athalin (1822) MMA.

238: *Frontispiece 1868 Edition of Gaspard de la Nuit*, etching by Félicien Rops (1868) NGA.

240 (top): *Two Grotesque Heads*, anonymous etching after Leonardo da Vinci (1640s) MMA.

240 (bottom): *A Man Making Water*, etching by Rembrandt (1630) MMA.

257: *Arriving Early*, collage by Bob Heman (2022).

258: *Louis Bertrand Dead*, drawing by David d'Angers (1841).

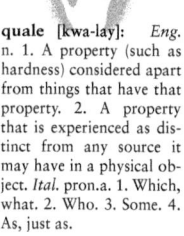

quale [kwa-lay]: *Eng.* n. 1. A property (such as hardness) considered apart from things that have that property. 2. A property that is experienced as distinct from any source it may have in a physical object. *Ital.* pron.a. 1. Which, what. 2. Who. 3. Some. 4. As, just as.

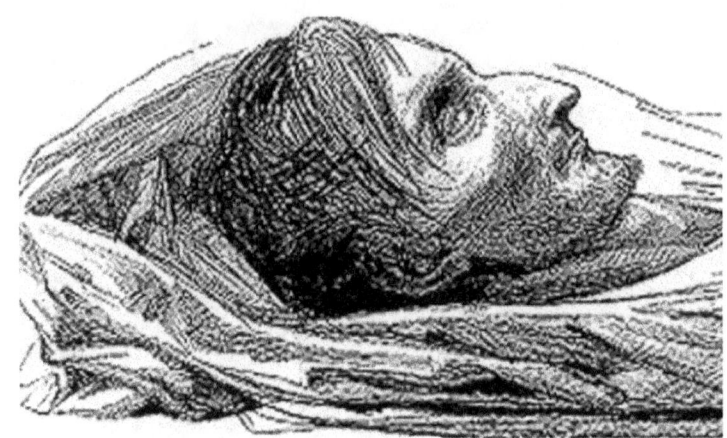

www.ingramcontent.com/pod-product-compliance
Lightning Source LLC
Chambersburg PA
CBHW080533170426
43195CB00016B/2548